Developing Thematic Units:
Process and Product

Developing Thematic Units: Process and Product

Diane D. Allen, Ed.D.
University of North Texas

Mary L. Piersma, Ed.D.
University of Alabama in Huntsville

Delmar Publishers
I(T)P An International Thomson Publishing Company

Albany • Bonn • Boston • Cincinnati • Detroit • London • Madrid
Melbourne • Mexico City • New York • Pacific Grove • Paris
San Francisco • Singapore • Tokyo • Toronto • Washington

NOTICE TO THE READER

Cover Design: Eva Ruutopold
Editing and Production: Graphic World Publishing Services
Composition: Graphic World, Inc.

Delmar Staff

Acquisitions Editor: Erin J. O'Connor
Project Editor: Colleen A. Corrice
Production Coordinator: Sandra F. Woods
Art and Design Coordinator: Timothy J. Conners

COPYRIGHT © 1995
By Delmar Publishers Inc.
an International Thomson Publishing Company
I(T)P™ The ITP logo is a trademark under license
Printed in the United States of America

For more information, contact:

Delmar Publishers Inc.
3 Columbia Circle, Box 15015
Albany, New York 12212-5015

International Thomson Publishing
Berkshire House
168-173 High Holborn
London, WC1V7AA
England

Thomas Nelson Australia
102 Dodds Street
South Melbourne 3205
Victoria, Australia

Nelson Canada
1120 Birchmont Road
Scarborough, Ontario
M1K 5G4, Canada

International Thomson Publishing
GmbH
Konigswinterer Str. 418
53227 Bonn
Germany

International Thomson Publishing
Asia
221 Henderson Bldg. #05-10
Singapore 0315

International Thomson Publishing
Japan
Kyowa Building, 3F
2-2-1 Hirakawa-cho
Chiyoda-ku, Tokyo 102
Japan

1 2 3 4 5 6 7 8 9 10 XXX 01 00 99 98 97 96 95 94

Library of Congress Cataloging-in-Publication Data

Allen, Diane D.
    Developing thematic units : process and product / Diane D. Allen,
Mary L. Piersma.
        p.   cm.
    Includes bibliographical references (p.) and index.
    ISBN 0-8273-6321-4
    1. Literature—Study and teaching (Elementary)
2. Interdisciplinary approach in education. 3. Education,
Elementary—Curricula. 4. Education, Elementary—Activity programs.
I. Piersma, Mary L. (Mary Lee), 1946- . II. Title.
LB1575A55 1995
372.64'043—dc20   94-17953
                                                                CIP

CONTENTS

PREFACE

The models presented in *Developing Thematic Units: Process and Product* were a result of the authors' work with undergraduate preservice elementary teachers. Texts that were available at the time addressed only thematic unit products. Rather than just producing a "product," that is, a thematic unit of study, the authors intend that undergraduate students would learn the "process" of developing thematic studies. With knowledge of the process, students would be able to develop their own products fashioned specifically for the elementary students in their future classes. These models and activities were later field-tested through workshops with elementary classroom teachers and administrators to gain feedback as to their usefulness in actual classroom settings.

Specifically, *Developing Thematic Units: Process and Product* is a handbook to help teachers (preservice and inservice) make connections between theory and practice in using children's literature across the curriculum. The handbook demonstrates three models of integrating children's literature into the elementary school curriculum and provides examples of the product to help bridge the gap between theory and practice.

A unique feature of this book is that it provides both preservice and inservice teachers with a step-by-step approach to the process of integrating literature, coupled with specific examples from science, social studies, and language arts.

By providing three different models that result from implementing the process, teachers can see that various options are possible and that utilizing this process provides a legitimate way of integrating literature into any curriculum area. Use of this process allows teachers to make sound decisions about using children's literature within the framework of mandated curriculum.

Special features of this book include:

1. A discussion of the research related to the use of children's literature in the classroom
2. A detailed outline of the process
3. Three unique examples resulting from using the process
4. A discussion of issues related to the use of literature in the classroom
5. Suggested topics and related books (children's literature)

This book is intended for use by preservice teachers in a university classroom setting or by inservice teachers in a workshop setting. This book is most useful for students who have prior knowledge of appropriate methodology, content, and children's literature for the elementary school child. It is an excellent complementary text for a reading or language arts course and can be used as a resource in building science or social studies units in those methodology courses.

ACKNOWLEDGMENTS

This book is the result of countless interactions with preservice teachers, inservice teachers, and children. It began as we collaborated to develop effective strategies in teaching our undergraduate methods classes at the University of Alabama in Huntsville. These experiences and our work with classroom teachers reaffirmed our belief that children learn best when engaged in authentic literacy experiences. Teachers and children continue to challenge us to refine our thinking about how children become literate.

We have been supported by numerous colleagues, friends, and students throughout the development of this text. Among our biggest supporters have been the faculties and staff at the University of North Texas and the University of Alabama in Huntsville. They have provided feedback as well as encouragement. Pam Lane, Vicki Sargent, and Jill Johnson at Hodge Elementary and Carol Hagen at the Child Development Lab at the University of North Texas in Denton provided wonderful opportunities to work with children and classroom teachers. Teachers and administrators who attended our workshops at regional and national conferences encouraged us to share our process, which they said gave them a framework to implement thematic units and encouragement to take risks. Erin O'Connor at Delmar saw promise in our initial manuscript and provided support as the final manuscript was developed. The comments of William S. Bingman (Frostburg State University, Frostburg, Maryland), Audrey H. Brainard (Hands-on-Science, Heathsville, Virginia), Eilene K. Glasgow (Pacific Lutheran University, Tacoma, Washington), Penelope R. Speaker (Tulane University, New Orleans, Louisiana), M. Kay Stickle (Ball State University,

Muncie, Indiana), and Norma Jean Strickland (Rust College, Holly Springs, Mississippi) helped us view our work from different perspectives and added new dimensions to the final draft. Shareen Scibek and Gary Miller helped with photography, conducted library research, and shared our enthusiasm.

Our purpose in writing this book was to encourage teachers to share the excitement of high-quality literature with their students. During the writing of this manuscript, we observed the enthusiasm of teachers and children as they shared literature across the curriculum. We are grateful to them for putting our theory into practice.

To our wonderful husbands and children.

—*D. A. & M. P.*

Developing Thematic Units: Process and Product

1

PERSPECTIVE

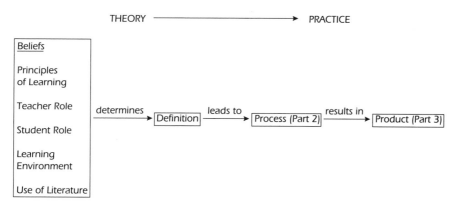

Figure 1.1 Graphic overview for Part One.

INTRODUCTION

Teachers at all levels are giving authentic children's literature a new priority in their classrooms. In the past, elementary teachers shared books with their students through read-aloud sessions or by requiring book reports and projects. However, with the growth of the whole language movement, teachers have begun to utilize literature in broader contexts and in more authentic ways across all levels of education. Students are engaged in reading self-selected books and responding to them in natural ways. Projects, reports, and book sharing stem naturally from students' involvement with **trade-books** and library books and from their own questions. The teachers and students in the following examples demonstrate how children's literature can be a resource in today's classrooms.

Example 1

Melinda and Jennifer are second-grade teachers in the same elementary school. At the beginning of the school year, they chose to substitute children's literature for the science and social studies textbooks. They chose high-quality literature, such as *Humphrey the Lost Whale* (Tokuda & Hall, 1986), *Big Al* (Yoshi, 1988), *Kermit the Hermit* (Peet, 1965), and *Going Lobstering* (Pallotta, 1990), that was rich in language but also allowed them to develop literature-based units that focused on major science and social studies concepts. For example, oceans provided the **focus** for one unit. Fiction and nonfiction books, magazines, and reference books were made available to the class. Children were encouraged to add to the collection from resources they might have at home. In response to reading and writing activities, children decided to demonstrate their knowledge by creating a room-sized aquarium filled with schools of colorful paper fish, a large stuffed oyster, a kelp forest, and a fifteen-foot replica of Humphrey the humpback whale. The students' creations were replicas of plant and animal life they had studied in the unit. They invited other classes to visit the aquarium and acted as tour guides, sharing their new knowledge about oceans.

Example 2

The first thing a visitor notices in Cheryl's fourth-grade classroom on this particular day is a group of children reading inside a large pagoda. Cheryl has borrowed books from both the school and public libraries, for example, *Many Lands, Many Stories: Asian Folktales for Children* (Conger, 1987) and *Chin Chiang and the Dragon's Dance* (Wallace, 1984). To this she has added from her own personal resources. These reading materials include books and magazines about Chinese art, poetry, folktales, and history. Traditional Chinese music permeates the room. Cheryl uses these resources to supplement her social studies unit on China and to make connections with other subject areas. The students study Chinese history, folklore, and geography in cooperative learning groups. Each group has chosen a "Chinese" name from the culture or history they are researching. As a part of their study, the children create a New Year's dragon and share their research reports with other classes as they parade through the school. Other activities include making fortune cookies, designing puppets, and creating Chinese lanterns and fans.

Figure 1.2 Second graders share resources in the library.

Figure 1.3 Parents contributed artifacts for unit on China.

Example 3

As part of their university coursework in an introductory reading methods class, a group of preservice teachers participated in the development of a unit based on Lois Lowry's *Number the Stars* (1989). The instructor began each day by reading aloud from the book, thus **modeling** oral reading. Questioning techniques and comprehension strategies that the future teachers might use in their own classrooms were modeled following each day's reading. The students kept literature response logs that included personal reflections on characters' actions, predictions about future events in the story, and comments on the German occupation of Denmark and other countries. Students created character sketches and character maps and illustrated their characters. Students also read an article in *The Reading Teacher* (1990) based on an interview with Lois Lowry and her experiences in preparing to write this book.

During the semester, students visited the public library to look for appropriate nonfiction and fiction to use with fourth and fifth graders in teaching this unit. They chose photo journals of events in Europe during the Nazi occupation, videos of the war, and children's literature with a similar theme, such as *Summer of My German Soldier* (Greene, 1973) and *Year of Impossible Goodbyes* (Choi, 1991). Students **brainstormed** possible activities for integrating curriculum into this unit of study. As a result of the brainstorming, they created a literature web showing how they might integrate reading this book with other content areas. The web included plans for reading literature written by Hans Christian Andersen, listening to Danish folk music, researching Jewish and Danish holiday traditions, doing historical research on the role of the Danes and Dutch in hiding Jewish families, and gathering general information on World War II.

Figure 1.4 Preservice teachers participate in literature response groups.

Although each of these settings is slightly different, each teacher made a conscious choice to use children's literature as a vehicle for developing **thematic units of study,** that is, learning experiences organized around a central focus. These teachers became decision makers about content, format, and resources; in turn, they were able to provide their students with choices that were relevant and that promoted higher-level thinking skills. By combining a variety of children's literature and other available resources, these teachers, at all educational levels, were able to develop thematic units of study that provided them with options for pursuing curriculum objectives and goals. The thematic units not only exposed the students to good pieces of literature but also made learning content relevant to their needs.

Developing Thematic Units: Process and Product was written in response to teachers' requests for guidance in the development of high-quality thematic units. Although a number of books and manuals are available to teachers, many of them are simply **prepackaged units** that do not encourage teachers to make choices relevant to their students and that may be in direct conflict with the philosophy of **literature-based instruction.** Instruction in literature-based—or whole language—classes requires units designed to meet the unique needs and interests of a particular learning community. This requirement can best be accomplished by a teacher and learners who work collaboratively in the classroom or by a collaborative group of teachers within the school. This text supports literature-based instruction by providing teachers with a process and with working models that can be used in the development of literature-based units tailored to the needs of their students and curriculum standards.

A BELIEF SYSTEM

The process developed for this text and modeled in it flows from the authors' beliefs about how children learn. Although these beliefs represent a general philosophy of learning, in this text they are applied specifically to the development of **literacy.** It is difficult to segment various aspects of a belief system; each aspect is intertwined completely with the other parts. To explain the various aspects of our beliefs about literacy development and growth and how they relate to classroom instruction, however, here we present and discuss five broad areas of our belief system: principles of literacy learning and instruction, the role of the teacher in literacy learning, the role of the student, the importance of environment in the promotion of literacy learning, and the use of literature-based instruction.

Presenting all of the research related to these ideas in this text would be impossible and perhaps undesirable. The reference sections at the end of the chapter will direct the reader to sources that provide support to the ideas

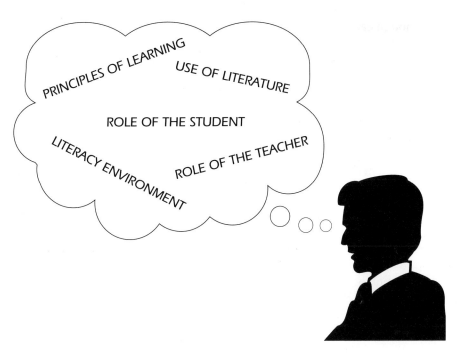

Figure 1.5 A belief system.

presented here. We hope that the following discussion will prepare the reader to understand the basis on which the remainder of the text is constructed.

Principles of Literacy Learning and Instruction

We begin this discussion of our belief system by outlining the basic tenets of our knowledge about how children become literate and the role that instruction plays in that development. These principles provide the framework for our belief system and the basis for developing our process of creating thematic units.

Principle 1

Literacy development is a natural process that should be considered as a "whole" process rather than bits and pieces of discrete skills. For example, when children are learning the oral language of their culture, they experiment with words, phrases, and clauses in a variety of situations. The child is not required to memorize discrete sounds of the oral language before being allowed to move along to pronouncing words. Instead, meaning is stressed from the beginning, and children learn that communication is the primary goal of language (K. Goodman, 1986). Likewise, knowledge about print is best learned in natural, holistic ways. Print should not be presented to children in small pieces that are removed from real contexts. Literacy instruction should stress the meaning and communication aspects of language (Goodman, 1986). Children need opportunities to practice, expand, and refine their knowledge of the language system in situations that support an integration of all aspects of language (speaking, listening, reading, and writing).

Principle 2

Children construct knowledge about language and literacy. At a very early age, children share responsibility for their own learning. They continuously explore and experiment with language. Children's literacy development begins with their oral language development. As children manipulate language, they develop new knowledge about how language operates and how meaning is constructed. For example, when an infant first says "ba ba" for bottle and receives the actual bottle from his mother, he begins to construct the knowledge that one function of language is to communicate needs. As adults we may think that these infant utterances are only one word, but they represent a complete thought: "Give me my bottle," for example. Children soon determine which sounds go together in their particular language to make meaning. They learn about structure, appropriateness, and function through experimenting with a variety of language options.

Children construct principles about how language works and revise their assumptions about how language works as they interact with the world around them. (This is particularly true about grammar and the structure of language.) If children are encouraged to experiment with oral language, they construct a knowledge base of generalizations that support their later learning of written language. The activities in which children are invited to participate should "encourage invention and constructive thinking" (Pace, 1991). When approaching a written text, children use this knowledge of language to experiment and to construct a meaning that combines their own **schema** with the information provided by the author. Children not only are interested in learning about literacy but also want to engage in it. They experiment with letters, words, signs, and symbols. They learn about language by using language. They are active

Figure 1.6 As kindergarten children participate in literacy centers that reflect real-life experiences, they construct their knowledge of language.

learners who engage in doing things, not learners who passively receive information.

Principle 3

Literacy development is enhanced through shared experiences. From Vygotsky's work (1962) we know that language learning is promoted through social relationships that make language meaningful. By interacting with others, children are able to experiment with new knowledge and confirm previously learned information. Classrooms should promote a sense of community to enhance literacy development and provide the necessary support for the creation of literacy skills. Learning to read, write, and respond to language must be embedded in real contexts at school, at home, and in communities that require children to interact with others. These tasks should not be reduced to discrete skills or removed from meaningful social contexts but should maintain the wholeness of language.

Principle 4

Literacy development is also personal and individual. Although shared experiences are vital to literacy growth, teachers should also remember that each child develops in a distinctly personal way. Children are individuals with diverse backgrounds, interests, and rates of development. Each child brings language, unique experiences, and understandings of concepts—a schema—to each task, and this background helps to determine what the child will learn from the task. Each child's unique experiences reflect that child's understanding of the surrounding world.

Principle 5

Learning, including knowledge about literacy, occurs when children engage in authentic experiences and activities. Children do more than complete worksheets, engage in writing based on teacher-determined topics and formats, or work on similar language drill activities; students engage in activities that are owned by the students because they are "useful, or interesting, or fun" (K. Goodman, 1986).

From Dewey's work we know that children need to be actively involved in an experience for learning to occur. This corresponds to Piaget's (Y. Goodman, 1990) theory that children must have an active role in their learning for knowledge to be acquired. When applying these theorists' ideas to language learning, Goodman (1986) tells us to "keep language whole and involve children in using it functionally and purposefully to meet their own needs" (p. 7). Language activities should be a natural outgrowth of a child's experimentaton with the language that is required for learning in all areas. Reading and writing should be real, not contrived. **Authentic experiences** and activities encourage children to draw upon their own personal experiences as they attempt to make sense of what they read and as they engage in their own writing. For example, rather than reading texts that have been written expressly for teaching reading skills, children should read authentic children's literature; instead of practicing writing friendly letters that are never mailed, children can compose letters of thanks to someone for a service or a gift or letters to pen pals and relatives. As Yetta Goodman (1988) explains, "It is only as students become actively engaged in wondering why and for what reasons people read and write and how such processes affect their own lives that they understand the power of language" (p. 263).

Children should be active participants in the learning process. They make choices and decisions about how they interact with one another and with print. They interact and collaborate with others in solving problems about literacy and about content material. They assume personal ownership and control of their own learning; that is, "they come to feel that they have the right to choose what they want to learn and to manage that learning in cooperation with their peers and teacher" (Cooper, 1993, p. 31).

Figure 1.7 Mailbox holds letters that students are mailing to pen pals.

Principle 6

A well-defined focus provides a framework that allows children to make connections among ideas, concepts, and experiences. When teachers develop thematic units of study, they create such a focus. Whether that focus is on a selection of literature or a more encompassing theme, students are more likely to understand why they are participating in an activity. Learning punctuation or grammar becomes meaningful if students see it in relation to the real world. For instance, the children in Example 1 might write letters to a marine biologist to ask questions about specific sea animals, or they could compose a brochure to use as a guide to their classroom aquarium. These types of activities illustrate how focused instruction can have real-world connections. In addition, a well-defined focus helps children see natural connections between the content (what they learn) and the process (how they learn). These connections should help children acquire an integrated knowledge base that is more meaningful for long-term learning. A well-defined focus makes learning "more closely attuned to the way children and adults learn" (Hughes, 1991).

Thematic units provide an avenue for the development and expansion of children's schemata. The broader and more developed a child's schema, the more likely the child is to construct complex understandings of written text. Goodman suggested that when teachers create units they are providing "a focal point for inquiry, for use of language, for cognitive development" (K. Goodman, 1986, p. 31).

Principle 7

Motivation is crucial to the development of positive attitudes about literacy. Children learn best when they want to learn and when they think they can learn (Bandura, 1977). They learn more readily when they are highly motivated and when the activities and experiences in which they participate are meaningful and purposeful (Holdaway, 1979). Sometimes motivation comes from within, but it may also be encouraged by the teacher, by other students, or even by activities.

Tangible rewards such as stickers or prizes are examples of **external motivation**. These types of rewards are initially motivating and may be necessary for some children; however, their effect is not longlasting. For independent learning, children must become internally motivated to learn. Of course, this is more difficult than it sounds; instead of stickers or bookmarks, teachers must provide an environment conducive to purposeful learning and an opportunity for it. Cooper (1993) suggests that motivation is "not a single activity that a teacher conducts; it involves a complete set of ongoing attitudes and activities that occur in the classroom environment and that lead to the creation of a community of learners including the teacher, who are excited about reading and writing and wanting to learn" (p. 31). **Internal motivation** occurs when children have some choices about what they are learning, how they are involved in the learning process, and how they are evaluated. Children soon develop a feeling of success if they are challenged and if they view the challenge as relevant to what they want to know. Knowing that they can successfully complete a task encourages children to investigate new areas and to take risks in their learning.

Role of the Teacher in Literacy Learning

The role of the teacher in a literature-based classroom differs from the role of the teacher in a **skills-based classroom.** The skills-based teacher can be characterized as a dispenser of knowledge, an evaluator of student products, and a manager of prescribed curricula. In contrast, a literature-based teacher decides to make choices about materials, **strategies,** and assessment. This teacher functions in a variety of roles.

Teachers themselves are readers and writers. They read and write when students are reading and writing. They engage in dialogue about what the children are reading and writing and share their love of reading. Teachers need to show students that they are themselves readers and writers, not just theorizers about reading and writing (Galda, Cullinan, & Strickland, 1993).

Teachers learn alongside the students. As students construct knowledge about concepts, teachers expand their own knowledge base. The students and teacher engage in research activities that expand their schema. The teacher gains new insights into literature from student responses and interactions. Teacher and students are members of a community of learners in which there is "high student input and high teacher input [where both] bring all of their skills, wisdom, and energy to the teaching/learning transaction" (Calkins, 1986, p. 165).

Teachers facilitate student learning. They provide students with opportunities for choice, input, and collaboration. They create an environment that encourages students to take risks in their learning and to become independent learners. The teacher acts as a "catalyst for problem solving, by creating the environmental conditions that support active learning" (Pahl & Monson, 1992, p. 519). Shared decision making gives students a sense of ownership.

Figure 1.8 Fourth graders are making decisions about which resources to use.

A literature-based teacher is...

- A reader and a writer
- A learner
- A facilitator of student learning
- A modeler of strategies
- A motivator
- An assessor of student progress
- A decision maker
- A collaborator with colleagues
- A communicator

Figure 1.9 Roles of a literature-based teacher.

Teachers model strategies for successful literacy experiences. The teacher must "provide demonstrations of the learning process and must model the use of meaning-making strategies" so that students can begin to coordinate and apply their learning in new contexts (Pahl & Monson, 1992, p. 519). The teacher demonstrates the use of selected strategies and provides scaffolding to support students as they begin to implement them. As they progress and gain confidence in the use of these strategies, the teacher monitors their progress and gradually releases the responsibility for learning until the students can successfully choose and independently implement appropriate strategies.

The teacher is a key factor in motivating students. Initially, motivation may be primarily external. The teacher creates an environment that supports active learning and provides the instructional scaffolding for problem-solving activities (Pahl & Monson, 1992). Often the teacher's own enthusiasm can stimulate the children's interest. The most important aspect of motivation is "modeling learning as a rewarding, fulfilling activity" (Wood, Bruner, & Ross, 1976). The results of this support ultimately lead the children to become increasingly self-motivated.

The teacher continuously assesses student progress. According to Au, Scheu, Kawakami, and Herman (1990), "The main purpose of assessment should be to provide teachers and students with information useful in promoting students' growth in literacy." The teacher uses a variety of assessment tools, such as observations, checklists, conferences, journals, and stu-

Figure 1.10 The teacher facilitates learning by modeling literacy behaviors.

dent projects to monitor student growth. **Authentic assessment** is embedded in the context of daily learning activities.

Teachers are actively involved in making instructional decisions. They make decisions about what will be taught, how it will be taught, which materials will be used, and how everything will be evaluated. By making these choices, teachers "purposefully and intentionally develop a method of enacting curriculum through which their engagement with teaching becomes explicit" (Sumara & Walker, 1991, p. 284). Teachers create and modify curriculum by making specific choices about grouping, time management, and appropriate resources.

Teachers work cooperatively with colleagues. They collaborate with colleagues at the same grade level and at other grade levels, with those in various subject areas, and with library media specialists. For instance, they can brainstorm ideas, plan activities, share resources, and reflect on their successes and failures. This collaboration allows teachers to develop units more quickly and with greater depth. Additionally, working closely with colleagues provides the teacher with moral and professional support. Teacher collaboration also benefits children.

The teacher's role as a communicator is crucial to success. Teachers must be able to articulate their beliefs concerning a literature-based program to administrators, colleagues, and parents. Informed administrators and parents are more likely to be supportive. Both administrators and parents should be invited to visit and to participate in classroom activities. Teachers should provide regular feedback to parents and administrators concerning class activities and student progress. Communication can help administrators understand the benefits of literature-based instruction, and parents can learn the importance of supporting their children's literacy growth.

Role of the Student in Literacy Learning

The role of the student in literacy learning in a literature-based classroom parallels that of the teacher; that is, the student is a reader, a writer, a learner, a collaborator, and so on. This role differs from that of a student in a skills-based classroom in several ways. Rather than being perceived as simply the recipient of knowledge, a student in a literature-based classroom participates in the construction of knowledge and in the sharing of knowledge. Such a student is actively involved in the process rather than passively accepting information. In a skills-based classroom, the student is often involved in completing worksheets, taking teacher-made tests, following directions, and experiencing only fragmented parts of literacy learning. In contrast, the student in a literature-based classroom makes choices about materials, resources, activities, and learning partners. Additionally, this student is often involved in **self-evaluation** and assessment and **peer evaluation** and assessment.

Many school districts in the United States are moving toward an **inclusion model** of special education in which special education students work with their peers in regular classrooms. In the classrooms described in this text, special education students are supported in their learning and become part of the learning team. Because instruction is more focused on the needs and interests of the students, these special students should find many opportunities to succeed.

Importance of Environment in Literacy Learning

Providing a nurturing environment, one that is rich in print and language (Morrow, 1992b), is a key factor in supporting children's literacy development in the classroom. The classroom environment should provide models of reading and writing, encouragement from adults and peers, and an abundance of accessible materials for reading and writing. All of these factors together make up an environment that encourages children in their exploration of language and literacy. Morrow's (1987) and Huck's (1993) research activities have demonstrated that an inviting classroom, particularly one with a well-designed library center, can lead to greater involvement of children in literacy activities. Many reading textbooks give excellent examples of classroom settings.

The classroom should have many books of varying levels and interests, books of general interest, books related to specific content areas of study, books "published" by the children, dictionaries, and other resource materials. Cullinan (1989) and Morrow (1985) stress the importance of including several types of children's literature at all reading levels, including picture concept books, fairy tales, nursery rhymes, picture story books, realistic literature, easy to read books, fables, folktales, informational books, biographies, newspapers, magazines, and poetry. For older children it is equally important to provide not only variety in fictional genres but also great variety in informational texts.

The materials available to children must reflect the fact that "literacy is context dependent" (Harste, Woodward, & Burke, 1984, p. 216) and include contexts such as journals, newspapers, poetry, environmental print (road signs, fast food signs, and product labels) personal letters, and catalogs. All of these kinds of print should be developmentally appropriate for the children in the classroom. The collections of reading material should be stored and displayed in such a manner that they invite children to select and enjoy something to read. Although many books are shelved with their spines facing outward, it is also important to display some books with the front cover facing outward. Such a technique draws attention and invites children to read these special books. Books featured in this manner should be changed frequently. The collections should also give evidence that the teacher values books and reading. Books chosen by the teacher for read-alouds are very often the books children later select for free reading. The collections on display should be changed frequently by borrowing from the school library or the public library and by including books shared by children or donated by parents. Organize the classroom collections of books in simple but useful categories. Devise a checkout system that the children can use. Young children can easily learn to write name, date, and book title on three-by-five-inch index cards and put the cards in alphabetical order. Intermediate children could design their own system and assist in carding and cataloging classroom book sets.

Although the actual collections of literature are important, they are not enough; the materials should be part of an inviting area in the classroom that encourages children to explore their own literacy and share reading material with others. Because the literacy centers are designed for children, the size and placement of all materials, including tables, chairs, and posters, should be appropriate for them. Centers should evolve as the classroom activities and even thematic units change. Children should be encouraged to help plan, manage, and clean literacy centers. Literacy-centered classrooms should have places for large and small group activities as well as for individual pursuits and personal privacy, such as a loft, a corner, a hideaway under an old desk, a private "office" created from an oversized carton, or even an old bathtub. Comfortable chairs like beanbags and rockers, pillows, tables, and soft rugs all help make a reading area inviting. Charts, posters, and book jackets created by children should have a prominent place on a nearby bulletin board. Posters that invite children to engage in literacy activities are available from the American Library Association (50 Huron Street, Chicago 60611), the Children's Book Council (67 Irving Place, New York 10003), and many school paperback clubs (Troll, Trumpet, Scholastic). Stuffed animals, puppets, dolls, cars, or trucks are all wonderful items to include in literacy classrooms; they are especially valuable if related to stories such as *Corduroy* (Freeman, 1968), *Madeline* (Bemelmans, 1939), *Humphrey the Lost Whale* (Tokuda & Hall, 1986), or *The Grouchy Ladybug* (Carle, 1977). Flannelboards, storyboards, and costumes should also be included to allow children to make up their own stories, retell old stories, or act out their favorite part of a book.

Figure 1.11 This display of books invites children to read.

Figure 1.12 Giant gingerbread man holds big books and activities for sharing.

Figure 1.13 Centers develop as themes change.

Figure 1.14 Bamboo hut provides a quiet place to read with a
friend.

Figure 1.15 *Children enjoy reading in a loft.*

Because reading and writing grow together, the learning environment should also include writing tools and a place to display children's writing. It should contain paper of many sizes, colors, and textures; pencils, markers, crayons, and chalk; scissors; and tape. Blank books, pictures, greeting cards, posters, and stickers can all be used to stimulate children to write and illustrate their own books. Tables and chairs to be used for writing, revising, or editing are a must. A typewriter and a computer with word processing programs should be included in this center. Many simple word processing programs are currently available for elementary school children (Appendix C). The area set aside for writing should also contain a place for children to organize and store their writing ideas and products. A simple folder or cubbyhole works well for this purpose. An area specially designed to assist children in publishing their work should also be available. It should contain a work surface as well as supplies children can use in creating their final product (cardboard, construction paper, wallpaper books, yarn, brads, and the like).

In an attempt to see the language arts as a whole, children should also have the opportunity to engage in listening and viewing activities. A tape recorder with headphones and a compact disc player, along with tapes

Figure 1.16 Children gather around the tree to share books with their friends, real and imaginary.

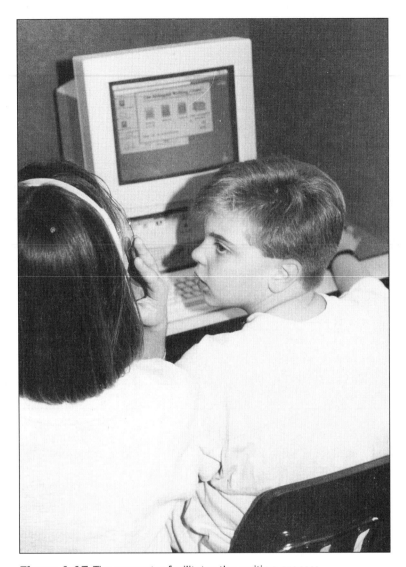

Figure 1.17 The computer facilitates the writing process.

of books and stories and blank tapes for students to record their own stories, should be located near the reading-writing area. Filmstrip viewers and video players also provide opportunities for children to experience literature and should be included in the environment. Video equipment might be used by children and teachers to create or document dramatic performance.

A learning environment that is conducive to literacy development is more than a collection of reading, writing, listening, and speaking materials. Literate, helping adults are central figures in this environment. Older children and adults, including parents and grandparents as well as the teacher, should read to children on a regular basis. Cox and Zarillo (1993) suggest that adults also need to help children in their search for meaning by answering children's questions and finding books that children request. They also have many opportunities to model successful reading and writing. Activities such as reading or writing notes, making lists, skimming a newspaper for information, reading a cookbook, or writing a letter give children a look at the authentic experiences of adults or older children in the real world. In addition, adults and older children may model appropriate behaviors of collaboration and cooperation to solve common problems or locate needed information. This personal attention and support make for a far richer learning environment.

Essential to the learning environment is the understanding that the environment in the classroom is emotionally safe. Because language and literacy development depend on the social interaction among the people in a classroom, it is important that children feel comfortable sharing their own work and commenting on the work of others. Children should not fear that their work will go unappreciated or that they will be ridiculed by others. The teacher should strive to create a community of learners who provide support to one another's learning.

Finally, one vital aspect in a literacy environment is often overlooked by teachers. That factor is time. A classroom filled with beautiful books, a variety of writing materials, and willing adults can create a love of literature and reading only if the children have sufficient time to read, respond to their reading, and share with others. Frequently, children in many of today's classrooms read only after they finish their other work: completing dittos, filling in blanks in workbooks, copying definitions, or reading aloud, for example (Anderson, Hiebert, Scott, & Wilkinson, 1985; Durkin, 1978–79; Goodlad, 1984).

Students need a time set aside to read without pressure to do something else. The teacher should plan a regularly scheduled time when children can browse and explore books as well as an uninterrupted time to read silently. Results of the National Assessment of Educational Progress (1980, 1981, 1982) show the value of regular, independent reading. Children who read

Figure 1.18 This child has just finished listening to his favorite story.

Figure 1.19 *A fifth grader shares a book with her first-grade reading buddy.*

the most, read the best. Certainly the time factor is a crucial part of a literate environment.

The literature environment itself is an important factor in the motivation of children within the literature program. It is vital to the development of oral language, the expansion of experience and knowledge, and the creation of an atmosphere that promotes real opportunities for reading and writing.

The Use of Literature-Based Instruction

The use of children's literature as a basis of instruction is congruent with the principles we hold about how children acquire literacy, the role of the teacher, and the importance of the classroom environment. Children's stories, poems, and nonfiction provide children with natural and authentic opportunities to experiment with, construct, and expand their knowledge about language and their world. Teachers can model specific strategies with children as they share experiences with their students in the study of a piece of literature. Students involved in a literature-based program learn that their responses to stories are valued and that several interpretations of stories are possible and even desired. Sharing discussions of plot, character, and setting with their peers and with adult participants helps children build self-confidence and literacy growth.

Before considering the integration of all content area subjects, teachers should first direct their attention to the integration of the language arts (speaking, listening, reading, writing); children's literature is the best way to achieve this integration (Routman, 1991). The next logical step is to look for avenues of pulling together the other areas of the curriculum. By using children's literature, teachers and students can build natural connections between content areas such as science, social studies, math, art, music, and drama.

Beyond connecting the various parts of the curriculum, research indicates that the use of literature also enhances students' reading achievement (Cohen, 1986; Eldredge & Butterfield, 1986; Holdaway, 1982). Gains in reading achievement have also been recorded in studies that focused on students who were considered poor readers (Chomsky, 1978; Fader, Duggins, Finn, & McNeil, 1976; Tunnell, 1986). Some studies also give evidence of improved attitudes about reading and enjoyment of it (Eldredge & Butterfield, 1986; Fader et al., 1976).

The use of literature in classrooms varies on a continuum from teacher choice and control to collaborative choices to independent student choice (Hiebert & Colt, 1989). The focus moves along a similar continuum from the use of a core book (selected by teacher for entire class) to literature units that support collaborative decision making to self-selection and pacing by the student (Zarillo, 1989). The models presented in this text offer teachers and students options at all points on this continuum. Sometimes the teacher may simply allow children to choose reading material to supplement and support a unit of study in a particular content area. Other times the teacher may choose to focus on one piece of literature that the entire class reads, discusses, and responds to. For a third option the teacher might choose to focus on a content area **concept,** with literature as the vehicle for presentation of information.

DEFINING *THEMATIC UNIT*

One way to integrate literature into the language arts and other content areas is through the development and implementation of thematic units. The idea for themed units grew out of the American Progressive Movement in the late 1800s, when educators began to advocate the use of projects to promote learning (Spodek, 1985). Their use has increased during this century. A recent survey reported that 50 percent of the teachers surveyed used themes or units frequently and that another 31 percent used them occasionally. Those two groups combined indicate that about 80 percent of the surveyed teachers were organizing much of their teaching around thematic units (Rowell, Alexander, & Kolker, 1993).

The term *thematic unit* frequently appears in today's professional literature. However, its meaning may vary from one source to another, depending on the author's perspective and purpose. The following examples illustrate some of the diversity represented in the literature.

> The true thematic unit will focus on a literary theme—an underlying idea that ties the characters, the setting, and the plot together. (Sippola, 1993, p. 222)

> A thematic unit is a framework based on a particular topic, idea, author, or genre. (Cooper, 1993, p. 63)

> Thematic units reflect patterns of thinking, goals, and concepts common to bodies of knowledge. They link together content from many areas of the curriculum and depict the connections that exist across disciplines. Thematic units provide a framework for a community of learners in which all children can continue to learn language and to construct knowledge. (Pappas, Kiefer, & Levstik, 1990, p. 49)

> A thematic unit is a method of organizing instructional time and materials around a topic which lends itself naturally to the integration of curriculum content areas. (Eisele, 1991, p. 53)

The perspective underlying *Developing Thematic Units: Process and Product* is unique because its purpose is to model the process of creating a thematic unit as well as to present a final product. In light of this perspective, it is important for the reader to know the authors' definition.

> A thematic unit is the result of a process in which learning experiences are organized around a central focus. The focus may be a piece of literature, a content area topic, or a set of integrated concepts and selections of children's literature.

This definition supports the idea that there is a legitimate place in the curriculum for each type of unit. In fact, choosing a different central focus allows the teacher and the students to use literacy for a variety of purposes. This definition also reflects the authors' assumptions that literacy develops naturally when children are encouraged to explore literature and construct their own meanings.

SUMMARY

In Part One we have presented a discussion that reflects our beliefs about children's literacy development, the roles of the teacher and student in supporting this development, the creation of a **literacy-rich environment,** and the use of a literature-based curriculum. From this theoretical base, we introduced a definition of "thematic units" that provides the framework for the remainder of the text. In the following pages, we provide a step-by-step process to assist the reader in moving from theory to practice.

REFERENCES CITED

Anderson, R. C., Hiebert, E. H., Scott, J. A., & Wilkinson, I.A.G. (1985). *Becoming a nation of readers: The report of the commission on reading.* Champaign: University of Illinois Center for the Study of Reading.

Au, K. H., Scheu, J. A., Kawakami, A. J., & Herman, P. (1990). Assessment and accountability in a whole literacy curriculum. *The Reading Teacher, 43,* 574–578.

Bandura, A. (1977). *Social learning theory.* Englewood Cliffs, NJ: Prentice Hall.

Calkins, L. M. (1986). *The art of teaching writing.* Portsmouth, NH: Heinemann.

Chomsky, C. (1978). When you still can't read in third grade: After decoding, what? In S. J. Samuels (Ed.), *What research has to say about reading instruction.* Newark, DE: International Reading Association.

Cohen, D. (1986). The effect of literature on vocabulary and reading achievement. *Elementary English 45,* 209–213.

Cooper, J. D. *Literacy: Helping children construct meaning.* New York: Houghton Mifflin.

Cox, C., & Zarillo, J. (1993). *Teaching reading with children's literature.* New York: Macmillan.

Cullinan, B. E. (1989). *Literature for young children.* Newark, DE: International Reading Association.

Durkin, D. (1978–79). What classroom observations reveal about comprehension instruction. *Reading Research Quarterly, 11,* 481–533.

Eisele, B. (1991). *Managing the whole language classroom.* Cypress, CA: Creative Teaching Press.

Eldredge, J. L., & Butterfield, D. (1986). Alternatives to traditional reading instruction. *The Reading Teacher, 40,* 32–37.

Fader, D., Duggins, J., Finn, T., & McNeil, E. (1976). *The new hooked on books.* New York: Berkeley.

Galda, L., Cullinan, B., & Strickland, D. (1993). *Language, literacy & the child.* New York: Harcourt Brace Jovanovich.

Goodlad, J. (1984). *A place called school.* New York: McGraw-Hill.

Goodman, K. (1986). *What's whole in whole language?* Portsmouth, NH: Heinemann.

Goodman, Y. (1988). Exploring the power of written language through literature for children and adolescents. *The New Advocate, 1,* 254–256.

Goodman, Y. (1990). *How children construct literacy.* Newark, DE: International Reading Association.

Harste, J., Woodward, V., & Burke, C. (1984). *Language stories and literacy lessons.* Portsmouth, NH: Heinemann.

Hiebert, E. H., & Colt, J. (1989). Patterns of literature-based reading instruction. *The Reading Teacher, 43,* 14–20.

Holdaway, D. (1979). *The foundations of literacy.* Sydney: Ashton Scholastic.

Holdaway, D. Shared book experience: Teaching reading using favorite books. *Theory into Practice,* 1982, *21,* 293–300.

Huck, C., Heplet, S., & Hickman, J. (1993). *Children's literature in the elementary school.* New York: Harcourt Brace Jovanovich.

Hughes, M. (1991). *Curriculum integration in the primary grades: A framework for excellence.* Alexandria, VA: Association for Supervision and Curriculum Development.

Lowry, L. (1990). Number the stars: Lois Lowry's journey to the Newberry award. *The Reading Teacher, 44,* 98–101.

Morrow, L. M. (1985). *Promoting voluntary reading in school and home.* Bloomington, IN: Phi Delta Kappa Educational Foundation.

Morrow, L. M. (1987). Promoting innercity children's recreational reading. *The Reading Teacher, 41,* 266–274.

Morrow, L. M. (1992b). *Literacy development in the early years: Helping children read and write* (2nd ed.). Boston: Allyn & Bacon.

National Assessment of Educational Progress. (1980). *Three national assessments of reading: Changes in performance, 1970–1980* (Report 11-R-01). Denver: Education Commission of the States.

National Assessment of Educational Progress. (1981). *Reading, thinking and writing: Results from 1979–1980 national assessment of reading and literature* (Report 11-L-01). Denver: Education Commission of the States.

National Assessment of Educational Progress. (1982). *Reading comprehension of American youth: Do they understand what they read? Results from the 1979–1980 national assessment of reading and literature* (Report 11-R-2). Denver: Education Commission of the States.

Pace, G. (1991). When teachers use literature for literacy instruction: Ways that constrain, ways that teach. *Language Arts, 68,* 12–25.

Pahl, M., & Monson, R. J. (1992). In search of whole language. *Journal of Reading, 45,* 518–524.

Pappas, C. C., Kiefer, B. Z., & Levstik, L. S. (1990). *An integrated language perspective in the elementary school.* White Plains, NY: Longman.

Routman, R. (1991). *Invitations: Changing as teachers and learners, K–12.* Portsmouth, NH: Heinemann.

Rowell, C. G., Alexander, J. E., & Kolker, B. (1993). Whole language practices: What's happening in the classroom? *Journal of Reading Education, 18,* 53–64.

Sippola, A. E. (1993). When thematic units are not thematic units. *Reading Horizons, 33,* 217–223.

Spodek, B. (1985). *Teaching in the early years.* Englewood Cliffs, NJ: Prentice Hall.

Sumara, D., & Walker, L. (1991). The teacher's role in whole language. *Language Arts, 68,* 276–285.

Tunnell, M. O. (1986). The natural act of reading: An affective approach. *The Advocate, 5,* 156–164.

Vygotsky, L. (1962). *Thought and language.* Cambridge, MA: MIT Press.

Wood, D., Bruner, J., & Ross, G. (1976). The role of tutoring in problem solving. *Journal of Child Psychology, 11,* 89–100.

Zarillo, J. (1989). Teachers' interpretations of literature-based reading. *The Reading Teacher, 43,* 22–28.

REFERENCES CONSULTED

Cullinan, B. (1987). *Children's literature in the reading program.* Newark, DE: International Reading Association.

Goodman, K. (1992). I didn't found whole language. *The Reading Teacher, 46,* 188–199.

Hayward, R. A. (1988). Inside the whole language classroom. *Instructor, 98,* 34–40.

Lipson, M. Y., Valencia, S. W., Wixson, K. K., & Peters, C. W. (1993). Integration and thematic teaching: Integration to improve teaching and learning. *Language Arts,* 252–263.

Morrow, L. M. (1992a). The impact of a literature-based program on literacy achievement, use of literature and attitudes of children from minority backgrounds. *Reading Research Quarterly, 27,* 251–275.

Newman, J. M., & Church, S. (1990). Myths of whole language. *The Reading Teacher, 44,* 120–126.

Oldfather, P. (1993). What students say about motivating experiences in a whole language classroom. *The Reading Teacher, 46,* 672–681.

Reutzel, D., & Cooter, R. B. (1992). *Teaching children to read: From basals to books.* New York: Merrill.

Ridley, L. (1990). Enacting change in elementary school programs: Implementing a whole language perspective. *The Reading Teacher, 44,* 640–648.

Routman, R. (1983). *Transitions: From literature to literacy.* Portsmouth, NH: Heinemann.

Tompkins, G. E. (1994). *Teaching writing: Balancing process and product* (2nd ed.). New York: Merrill.

Tompkins, G. E., & Hoskisson, K. (1987). *Language arts: Content and teaching strategies* (2nd ed.). New York: Merrill.

Trelease, J. (1985). *The read aloud handbook.* New York: Penguin Books.

Tunnell, M. O., & Jacobs, J. S. (1989). Using "real" books: Research findings on literature based reading instruction. *The Reading Teacher, 42,* 470–477.

CHILDREN'S LITERATURE CITED

Bemelmans, L. (1939). *Madeline.* New York: Simon and Schuster.

Carle, E. (1977). *The grouchy ladybug.* New York: Crowell.

Choi, S. N. (1991). *Year of impossible goodbyes.* New York: Dell.

Conger, D. (1987). *Many lands, many stories: Asian folktales for children.* Rutland, VT: Tuttle.

Freeman, D. (1968). *Corduroy.* New York: Viking.

Greene, B. (1973). *Summer of my German soldier.* New York: Bantam.

Lowry, L. (1989). *Number the stars.* New York: Dell.

Pallotta, J. (1990). *Going lobstering.* Watertown, MA: Charlesbridge.

Peet, B. (1965). *Kermit the hermit.* Boston: Houghton Mifflin.

Tokuda, W., & Hall, R. (1986). *Humphrey the lost whale.* Union City, CA: Heian.

Wallace, I. (1984). *Chin Chiang and the dragon's dance.* New York: Atheneum, 1984.

Yoshi. (1988). *Big Al.* New York: Scholastic.

PROCESS

THE PROCESS APPROACH TO UNIT PLANNING

Select a Model

| Supplemental | Infused | Centered |
| FOCUS | FOCUS | FOCUS |

BRAINSTORM

(knowledge - concepts)

CONSULT LOCAL CURRICULUM GUIDES

LOCATE RESOURCES

CREATE A WEB

(Integrate brainstorming and curriculum guides)

FORMULATE UNIT OBJECTIVES

ORGANIZE ACTIVITIES

EVALUATE

Figure 2.1 Graphic overview for Part Two.

INTRODUCTION

In building (planning) units of instruction that maximize the use of children's literature, teachers must make some important decisions. This chapter leads teachers through the decision-making process as illustrated in the graphic overview to Part Two.

SELECT A MODEL

Research shows that individual teachers plan units with different purposes in mind. A teacher might learn of a new book and want to plan a unit of instruction around it. A first-grade teacher might choose to develop a unit on the topic of communities and use literature as a supplement. A teacher might also plan a unit on the environment that lends itself to integrating social studies, science, math, art, and language arts. Each of these units is different, and each gives the teacher a legitimate option in planning for specific purposes. Each of these represents one of three models for unit planning.

Model 1, referred to as the *literature supplement model*, uses literature as a supplement to content area instruction. In this model, teachers would provide tradebooks to enhance the study of a topic such as space, animals, or communities. Although a large variety of books on the topic are available to the children in the classroom, the teacher spends little instructional time with the books. Students use the books as resources for reports and projects or just as recreational reading.

Model 2, the *literature-centered model*, begins with a specific piece of literature such as *The Hungry Caterpillar* (Carle, 1969), *From Anna* (Little, 1972), *Sylvester and the Magic Pebble* (Steig, 1969), or *Number the Stars* (Lowry, 1989), which the children read or have read to them. Instruction focuses on story elements such as plot, characters, and setting and on the students' responses to the literature. However, the teacher also looks for opportunities to help children make connections with other areas they are studying. For example, in using *Sylvester and the Magic Pebble* (Steig, 1969), a teacher might help the children relate this story to science by having them sort and classify rocks according to size or to math by having them measure the rocks. With *The Hungry Caterpillar* (Carle, 1969), the children might study the life cycle of a butterfly, nutrition, or counting. *From Anna* (Little, 1972) could provide opportunities for the teacher to address handicapping conditions and the feelings and needs related to them. The teacher might also have the children study families or the emotions related to moving.

Model 3, the *literature-infused model*, represents a balance between the use of children's literature and concepts selected from all content areas. Although this model is the most complicated in its planning and implementation, it probably offers the most benefits to teachers and children. This model requires the teacher to use children's literature to teach the concepts, skills, attitudes, and values from the selected content areas. By using literature in this way to make connections between areas, children can see how science is related to social studies, social studies is related to math, and art is related to both, for example.

Step 1

In this and subsequent examples, follow Dorothy as she proceeds through the process of creating a thematic unit.

Dorothy teaches third grade in an urban elementary school. She has twenty-six students, eleven girls and fifteen boys.

At this first step of the process, Dorothy has decided to develop a thematic unit that is literature centered (model 2).

Figure 2.2 Select a model.

The initial step in planning a unit of instruction is to select one of these models to meet a specific purpose. Throughout the school year, the teacher has the opportunity to use each of these models. The teacher may want to start a collection of thematic units by developing several of the literature supplement model or the literature-centered model to begin the school year. The development of the literature-infused model is more demanding and is best accomplished when two or more teachers and/or students work together. Perhaps all teachers at one level—for example, second grade—could collaborate to develop one or two units a year. Although any of these models can be developed by the individual teacher, the process is enhanced when more minds work together to share ideas and activities.

CHOOSE A FOCUS

Once the model has been selected, the teacher is ready to choose a focus for the unit. A teacher who chooses model 1 (literature supplement) can select a topic from any content area. This topic could be based on the curriculum guide, the text, or teacher or student interest. For example, the teacher might want to do a science unit on plants or a social studies unit on families. The teacher then selects a variety of literature—both fiction and nonfiction—that will supplement the topic being studied.

If the teacher selects model 2 (literature-centered), the focus of instruction is a single piece of literature. The teacher will want to select a book or books that are age appropriate in theme and interest for the students in the classroom. After a selection has been made, the teacher reviews the chosen books and looks for opportunities to relate other content areas to this book through instructional activities. The teacher must also decide if the book will be read aloud to the children or if each child will read independently. If the children are reading on their own, sufficient copies of the book should be available.

If the teacher chooses model 3 (literature-infused), the focus is on a combination of concepts from several content areas and from selected tradebooks for children. The teacher initially determines the subject concepts and

---

Step 2

Dorothy looked at several pieces of literature that she thought her students would enjoy. She chose *Sarah, Plain and Tall* by Patricia MacLachlan for a number of reasons. First, it represented good, high-quality literature, and she knew the story was one the students would enjoy. Second, the readability and interest levels were appropriate for her students. Last, she knew that the book would provide good background information for a later social studies unit on westward expansion.

Figure 2.3 Choose a focus.

through the unit planning process identifies which pieces of children's literature are appropriate for teaching those concepts.

BRAINSTORM

After selecting the focus, the next step in the process of unit building for all models is to brainstorm all related ideas. Brainstorming is a creative process in which all ideas, no matter how absurd or ridiculous they may seem, are written down. If this is a group effort of several teachers, students, or a mixed group, the list of ideas is broader and longer. Shared knowledge increases the likelihood that the unit will have variety and a depth of activities.

1. On a piece of paper, write the focus.
2. Ask yourself some of the following questions:
   a. What concepts should be taught?
   b. What literature might be appropriate?
   c. What activities could the students do?
   d. How can we make this book come alive?
   e. What can we do to make this unit really creative?
3. Record all ideas. Be creative. Do not eliminate ideas that may seem unusual or impossible to implement. Focus on quantity rather than quality; refinement will come later. At this point, sequencing and order are not important. The more ideas you generate, the greater the potential for a successful unit.

Step 3

Dorothy wrote down all the ideas she could think of for activities and lessons.

family values	videos
history	reader's theater
letter writing	dioramas, murals
map skills	visitors
tracing journey	crafts - weaving - quilts
churning butter	folk songs
step-parents	beef jerky
characterization	listening
clothing	outlining reports
visit museums	enjoyment

Figure 2.4 Brainstorming.

CONSULT CURRICULUM GUIDES

Sometimes local or state-**mandated curriculum** guidelines discourage teachers from using literature-based instruction. Teachers feel bound to teach only specific concepts and skills by using only state-adopted textbooks. Literature-based thematic units of study, however, provide many opportunities to extend or enhance the teaching and learning of those concepts identified in local or state curriculum guides.

The curriculum guide is an important resource for the teacher who wants to build thematic units of study. The teacher should review the concepts for the grade level. For those teachers using model 1, concepts related specifically to the topic and content area should be listed. Model 2 focuses on literature; therefore, the teacher should look primarily for language arts concepts that could be addressed with the selected piece of children's literature but also identify related concepts in other subject areas. Model 3 requires the greatest use of the curriculum guide; the teacher must look for a variety of objectives and concepts from several content areas. Our suggestion for Model 3 is that, initially, all areas of the curriculum should be researched for appropriate concepts and skills to be taught. Motivating and previously unidentified areas that could be used in the unit might emerge.

LOCATE RESOURCES

The next step in the process of developing thematic units is to compile a list of possible resources for the unit. It is important to know what items or activities are available and what conditions must be met to obtain them. Of primary importance is the list of children's literature. For model 1 the teacher will want to locate supplemental books at a variety of reading levels. The children will use these books to expand their understanding of the content and as resources for reports and projects. The teacher who has chosen to create a model 2 unit will want to ensure that enough copies of the selected book are available for the entire time period. With model 3, the teacher locates books that will enable students to explore the theme and investigate concepts. Again, the teacher should be sure to include books at a variety of reading levels so that each child has the opportunity to find a book. Possible sources of books include the public library, the school library, the classroom library, and the personal libraries of the teacher and the students.

Once the literature has been located, the teacher is ready to investigate potential sources of additional materials. Other types of resources include magazines and newspapers; videos, films, and filmstrips; computer games and programs; maps, charts, and graphs; manipulatives and science equipment; parents and other community members; field trip possibilities; puppets; and

Step 4

Dorothy next consulted her district and state curriculum guides to see what concepts she might incorporate into her unit. She considered the following areas: language arts, social studies, art, music, math, and possibly science. After searching the curriculum guides, she decided to integrate the following concepts.

Language arts
- Draw inferences and conclusions
- Determine main idea of a passage
- Use context clues to determine word meanings
- Confirm predictions by locating specific details
- Ask relevant questions
- Develop and write paragraphs with topic sentences
- Proofread own writing for errors
- Continue understanding of character development and story structure
- Write friendly letters
- Correctly address envelopes

Social studies
- Families
- Importance of values
- Use of and dependence on natural resources
- Passage of time
- Locational skills related to maps and globes

Art and music
- Sing songs related to units of study
- Participate in folk dances
- Create murals and collages
- Visit local museums and galleries

Math
- Measure distances
- Work with temperature
- Solve word problems about time
- Interpret maps, globes, and charts

Science
- Uses of soil
- Conservation of soil
- Machines

Figure 2.5 Consult curriculum guides.

records and tapes. Many times the teacher can locate useful items by surveying parents and other teachers.

All literature and resources should be evaluated carefully in order to maintain high quality. Care should be taken to ensure that book choices reflect the best available literature. Figures 2.7 and 2.8 are sample checklists for evaluating fiction and **informational texts.** Books that promote commercial products and characters should be avoided. Business and industry can be rich resources for other types of educational materials; however, these should be carefully screened to eliminate any that simply promote the product.

CREATE A PLANNING WEB

Creating a **planning web** encourages the teacher to look at the total picture, to ask which of these concepts and activities can be pulled together to create a workable unit, and to make a final selection of resources. First, the teacher should select a limited number of curriculum concepts and skills that are appropriate and can be addressed within the constraints of time, resources, and interest. Next, activities, concepts, and ideas from the brainstorming activity are matched to the list of concepts and skills from the curriculum guides.

Step 5

Because Dorothy was creating a unit whose focus was *Sarah, Plain and Tall*, she wanted to ensure that she had enough copies of that book for all twenty-six students. Through the school library, the public library, and other teachers, Dorothy located twenty copies of the book. She decided to purchase six additional copies of the book, which she would later add to her classroom library.

Among the other resources that Dorothy located to use with this unit were (1) a video of the made-for-television movie; (2) a taped interview with author Patricia MacLachlan, which Dorothy ordered from a book club; (3) large maps of the United States and globes of the world; and (4) records, tapes, and diskettes of American folk songs.

Dorothy previewed all materials. The movie and interview were of the highest quality and were recommended by experts in the field of children's literature. Dorothy eliminated several of the songs on one record because they presented stereotypical views of Native Americans.

Figure 2.6 Locate resources.

Evaluation Checklist for Children's Narrative Text

Criteria	Present (y/n)

1. Setting
    a. Believable
    b. Authentic
    c. Familiar (for young children)
2. Characters
    a. Actions and behaviors believable
    b. Consistent
    c. Behaviors appropriate for age and background
3. Plot
    a. Beginning: prepares reader for action
    b. Middle: has conflict or problem
    c. Ending: climax or resolution
    d. Subplots (for older children)
    e. Character action aids development
4. Theme
    a. Appropriate to age or developmental level of child
    b. Implicit rather than explicit
5. Illustrations
    a. Contribute to or enhance story line
    b. Age appropriate

Recommendations and awards:

Figure 2.7 Evaluation checklist for narrative text.

Added to these are the literature and resources that have been located. Once these concepts, activities, and pieces of literature have been identified, the teacher is ready to create a web that will show potential connections between concepts, activities, and literature. When the web is complete, the teacher has an overview of the entire thematic unit and can then develop a rubric to ensure a connection between concepts and activities.

FORMULATE UNIT OBJECTIVES

Once the teacher has established a clear picture of both concepts and literature and has reflected on the connections to be made, it is time to plan actual teaching goals and objectives. They should address the areas of knowledge, processes, and attitudes and values. This is one of the most crucial

Evaluation Checklist for Children's Informational Text

Criteria	Present (y/n)

1. Presents accurate information
2. Presents a balanced view
3. Provides current information
4. Text supported by charts, maps, and/or tables
5. Organizes information in logical or sequential manner
6. Author possesses appropriate qualifications

Recommendations and awards:

Figure 2.8 Evaluation checklist for informational text.

Step 6

   Dorothy created the following web. It includes some of her brainstorming ideas, selected concepts and skills from the district third-grade curriculum guide, and the additional resources she located.

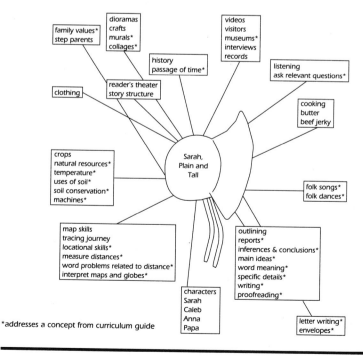

Figure 2.9 Create a planning web.

Organizational Chart

Theme: _____

Activities	Language Arts	Science	Social Studies	Math	P.E.	Art
Initiating Activities						
1.						
2.						
3.						
Developing Activities						
1.						
2.						
3.						
4.						
Concluding Activities						
1.						
2.						
3.						

Figure 2.10 Method for documenting connections between content areas.

aspects of planning thematic units because it gives direction and organization to all of the creative work that has already taken place. This step can also give teachers confidence that they are really meeting the needs and interests of the children and at the same time meeting the demands of mandated curriculum.

ORGANIZE ACTIVITIES

At this point the teacher sequences the activities from the web. Sequencing these activities provides the means to meet the chosen objec-

Step 7

Dorothy reviewed the web she had created to organize the concepts, skills, and activities she needed to teach with the literature for this unit. Then she developed **knowledge objectives, process objectives, and attitude objectives** to provide an outline for the instructional activities for this unit. Some examples from each category are provided below.

Knowledge
Students will learn:

- The main characters of a story are central to the action. The main characters in this story are Sarah, Caleb, Anna, and Papa. The students will be able to identify and describe the main characters of *Sarah Plain and Tall*.
- A friendly letter consists of a heading (date and return address), a greeting, the body of the letter, the closing, and the signature.
- An envelope for a friendly letter should include the address of the recipient in the center, the return address in the upper left corner, and the correct postage in the upper right corner. The address of the recipient includes name, street address, city, state, and zip code.

Process
Students will:

- locate specific states on a map or globe
- calculate the distance between two places on the globe or map
- solve word problems related to distance
- use context clue strategies to determine unknown words

Attitude
Students will:

- demonstrate cooperative effort in the development of projects
- demonstrate an appreciation for the musical heritage of pioneering Americans

Figure 2.11 Formulate unit objectives.

tives. These activities are sequenced into three groups: initiating, developing, and concluding activities. The initiating activities should be those that set the stage and create an interest in the unit. Developing activities provide the bulk of the activities in the unit. Last, concluding activities provide closure to the unit and allow students to apply what they have learned.

EVALUATE

When teachers think of evaluation in relation to a particular unit of study, end-of-the-unit tests usually come to mind first. Assessing students' progress at the end of the unit is important; however, the teacher who values all types of learning should consider evaluation in much broader terms. Not only should students be evaluated but also the effectiveness of the unit and of the instruction should be determined.

Step 8

Dorothy again reviewed her web to retrieve the activities listed there. Using these activities and the objectives she had just formulated, Dorothy determined which of the activities would be best used as initiating, or introductory, activities; which would provide the majority of the instruction; and which would help bring closure to the unit. The following are examples of some activities Dorothy developed through this process.

Initiating Activities

To begin this unit, Dorothy decided to talk about families. The first activity would begin with a brainstorming session in which the children each contributed different ways families are organized, such as father, mother, child, and child; mother and child; and grandparent and child; stepfather, mother, and child. The children would then each write a paragraph about their families to be included in a class book titled *Our Families*.

Developing Activities

1. The children would write friendly letters to a member of their families, preferably someone who lived in another city or town.
2. In small groups the children would create a mural depicting Sarah's town on the Maine coast and her new home on the prairie.

Concluding Activity

The children will share the group reports they have written about life on the prairie.

Figure 2.12 Organize activities.

Unit Effectiveness

Throughout the unit of study, the teacher should be evaluating the effectiveness of particular activities and instruction. Continuous evaluation of this type allows the teacher to reteach some sections or to readjust the activities for a particular student's needs. At the end of the unit, the teacher should spend some time reworking the unit to discard inappropriate activities or to add new activities that were created or discovered during the unit. This could be based on the rubric developed from the planning web. New resources that became available or that would have been helpful during the unit should be noted.

Student Progress

Evaluation of student progress should be threefold: **teacher evaluation,** peer evaluation, and self-evaluation. The teacher can evaluate students' knowledge and application of skills through the use of teacher-made tests. Projects and reports offer other means of evaluating students. The teacher could develop checklists to facilitate recording information relevant to goals, objectives, and outcomes.

During group work, students should have the opportunity to evaluate the work of individuals within the group and the work of the group as a whole. This is most easily completed through either checklists or summary statements at the end of each session of group work. (See examples in Part Three.)

Students are not traditionally requested to evaluate their own work. However, students who are to become independent learners must develop the skills required for critical judgment of their own efforts. **Learning logs** or journals give students the opportunity to describe their work and reactions to it in a narrative form. At the end of the unit, these log entries could be reviewed and pertinent statements could be highlighted. A student could then write a final evaluation report and substantiate it with statements from the logs.

Portfolio assessment as an alternative to standard measures could provide opportunities to include all three areas of student evaluation. A student progressing through the unit should collect artifacts to include in the portfolio. They might include reports, reading logs, group checklists, teacher checklists, student reactions to discussions or activities, and reference notes, among other things. A teacher-student conference at strategic points would guide the student in selecting activities and in addressing specific areas of concern regarding the student's work. Teachers would be able to monitor more closely the progress of each student as well as the effectiveness of the instruction.

Step 9

Dorothy had successfully used portfolio assessment with her reading program. She decided to expand its use for this unit. She asked students to include specific checklists and learning logs. Also, she asked the students to include work that they thought was representative of their learning during this unit.

Dorothy had previously developed checklists to help students evaluate their work in cooperative learning groups. Those checklists were adapted for use with this unit. She developed new checklists that listed the objectives and goals of this unit so that she could keep track of student learning and progress. Finally, she and the students together developed a checklist that could be used to indicate progress on particular unit-long projects, such as the murals.

Twice during the unit Dorothy scheduled a conference with each student. The purpose of the conference was to review the portfolio and evaluate the work to that point. Students were allowed to explain and interpret the artifacts they had included in the portfolio.

Dorothy planned to keep her own log of each day's activities and reactions. This log would help her evaluate the unit's success or failure at the end of this three-week unit.

Figure 2.13 Evaluation.

SUMMARY

In Part Two we outlined the specific process for developing thematic units. Three models of units were presented. The literature supplement model uses literature to support and expand a content unit of study. The literature-centered model focuses on the enjoyment of a single piece of literature. However, the teacher also uses the text to illustrate or expand concepts from one or more subject areas. Finally, the literature-infused model combines literature and content area concepts to provide connections among several areas of study. It is important to remember that all of these models provide valid means of instruction. In Part Three detailed examples of each of these models are presented.

CHILDREN'S LITERATURE CITED

Carle, E. (1969). *The hungry caterpillar*. New York: Philomel Books.

Little, J. (1972). *From Anna*. New York: Harper & Row.

Lowry, L. (1989). *Number the stars*. New York: Dell Publishing.

MacLachlan, P. (1985). *Sarah, plain and tall*. New York: Trumpet.

Steig, W. (1969). *Sylvester and the magic pebble*. New York: Trumpet.

PRODUCT

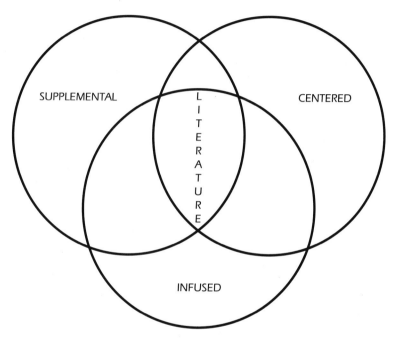

Figure 3.1 Graphic overview for Part Three.

Literature as a Supplement to Content Teaching

LIFE WEST OF THE MISSISSIPPI IN THE 1800s

Model

The model used for the development of this unit is literature as a supplement to content learning. In this model the textbook is the starting point for instruction. The tradebooks, reference books, media, and human resources may be chosen by either the teacher or the students and are used as supplementary resources to the text and to the learning activities.

Focus

The focus for this unit is the study of daily life in the western United States during the 1800s. It begins with the Louisiana Purchase and the exploration of that territory by Lewis and Clark. This was the time of exploration by white Americans, their treaties and conflicts with Native Americans, the opening of territory to homesteaders, the gold rush, and the growth of intercontinental travel. Most commercial social studies series also include the Civil War in this unit. However, that war is not addressed in this unit.

This unit follows the movement of white settlers into the vast western territories and examines their daily lives. Pioneer lives were affected by the conditions of the land and by the people with whom they came in contact. They might include Native Americans, trappers and hunters, soldiers, outlaws, miners, traveling salesmen and showmen, and immigrants. In turn, the pioneers had an impact on those whose hunting grounds and tribal lands they overran.

This unit could be adapted for use at fourth-, fifth-, or sixth-grade levels. Westward expansion is generally addressed during the fifth-grade year in most published social studies series, which is therefore the targeted grade for this presentation.

The resources for this unit are vast. The unit could conceivably take as long as nine weeks; however, three to four weeks would be suitable.

Brainstorming

The ideas and concepts presented in Figure 3.2 are the result of brainstorming the topic of daily life in the West during the 1800s. By encouraging student participation in the brainstorming activity, the teacher gains information about students' prior knowledge, misconceptions, and interests.

wilderness	Pony Express
territories	missions
gold rush	*Little House on the Prairie*
pioneer	folk songs
Beckworth	Indian Territory
courage	Black Kettle
exploration	pueblos
mountains	tepees
survival	museums
stagecoach	*Sourcebooks of the*
Oregon Trail	*American West*
outlaws	Native Americans
cowboys	Louisiana Purchase
square dancing	manifest destiny
homesteaders	sod houses
railroads	map skills
buffalo	trail bosses
Bill Cody	villages and towns
Texas Rangers	Chief Joseph
Chinese laborers	soldiers
plains	Little Big Horn
Lewis and Clark	49ers
covered wagons	*Sarah Plain and Tall*
log cabins	legends
trappers	*Legend of the Bluebonnet*
lawmen	ponies, mustangs
Jefferson	Wounded Knee
treaties	weaving, basketry
transportation	buffalo soldiers

Figure 3.2 Social studies ideas from brainstorming.

CURRICULUM GUIDES

The goals listed next are representative of specific goals listed for the study of social studies in the fifth grade.

Students will learn:

1. Similar needs of people in various cultures
2. Group and individual contributors to our culture
3. The role of tradition in our culture
4. Geographical features of the western United States
5. Land forms
6. Human and natural resources
7. The role of hunters and trappers
8. The concept of geographical dependency
9. Important historical events related to the westward expansion of the 1800s
10. Transportation needs related to western expansion
11. Effects of past events on our lives today
12. The use of special-purpose maps
13. The recording of and use of data on graphs, charts, and tables
14. The application of directional skills related to map reading

Resources

Resources for this unit range from the required textbook to the supplemental resources of books and audiovisuals. A list of those resources chosen for this unit follows. Some of the resources are more appropriate for teachers' use as background information; they may choose to share portions of them with students. Resources on this topic are numerous; therefore, what is listed here should be considered only a sample of what is available. Each teacher should feel free to add or subtract materials, depending on the availability of resources and the interests and abilities of students.

All commercial textbooks for the fifth grade include a unit or chapters that would be appropriate for this unit. For this specific example, *America's History* by Bonnie B. Armbruster, Charles L. Mitsakos, and Vincent R. Rogers was chosen. This text was published by Ginn & Company in 1987.

Other resources for this unit include the June 1988 issue of *Cobblestone Magazine* and the computer simulation game called *Oregon Trail*. A teacher living in an area with one or more museums should investigate to determine whether there are exhibits the students could visit that would expand their understanding of pioneer life. There may also be human resources that may contribute specific knowledge and skills to the class or groups of students.

A list of teacher resources is presented next; a supplemental reading list for students follows the teachers' list. Both narrative and expository texts are included, as well as books at a variety of reading levels and interests. Some of these books have early publication dates and may be difficult to locate; however, they offer excellent information and are worth the effort to find. A brief annotation is given for each student text.

TEACHER RESOURCES
Books

Bradbury, J. (1986). *Travels in the interior of America in the years 1809, 1810, and 1811*. Lincoln, NE: University of Nebraska.

Brown, D. A. (1970). *Bury my heart at Wounded Knee*. New York: Holt, Rinehart & Winston.

DeVoto, B. (1980). *Across the wide Missouri*. Boston: Houghton Mifflin.

Drumm, S. M., Ed. (1982). *Down the Santa Fe Trail and into Mexico: The diary of Susan Shelby Magoffin, 1846–1847*. Lincoln, NE: University of Nebraska.

Egan, K. (1988). *Teaching as storytelling: An alternative approach to teaching and the curriculum*. London: Rutledge.

Hungry Wolf, B. (1980). *The ways of my grandmothers*. New York: Morrow.

Katz, W. L. (1987). *The Black West*. Seattle: Open Hand Publishing.

Smith, A. M. (1992). *Ute tales*. Salt Lake City, UT: University of Utah Press.

Unruh, J. D. (1982). *The plains across: The overland emigrants and the trans-Mississippi west 1840–1860*. Champaign: University of Illinois Press.

Vine, D. J. (1974). *Behind the trail of broken treaties*. New York: Dell.

Weatherford, J. M. (1991). *Native roots: How the Indians enriched America*. New York: Crown.

White, J. I. (1975). *Git along little dogies: Songs and songmakers of the American West*. Urbana: University of Illinois Press.

Teaching Kits

United States Expands: 1785–1842. This is a teaching package developed from archives and includes documents and slides. SIRS, Inc., P.O. Box 2348, Boca Raton, FL 33427-2348. Cost: $40.00.

The California Goldrush: 1849. (Order #R-A3.) This packet includes posters, news accounts, and maps. Jackdaw Publishers, P.O. Box A03, Amawalk, NY 10501. Cost: $21.95.

SUPPLEMENTAL READING LIST FOR STUDENTS
Books

Alter, J. (1989). *Growing up in the old West.* New York: Franklin Watts.
   This book outlines and describes such events in the 1840s through 1890s as life in a covered wagon, prairie homes (sod, cabins), chores, play and games, school, and natural and manmade disasters and dangers.

Alter, J. (1989). *Women of the old West.* New York: Franklin Watts.
   When we think of women on the prairie, we usually think only of the homesteading wife and mother. This book gives examples of other types of women who helped to settle the West. These include laundresses, army officers' wives, teachers, doctors, lawyers, actresses, reformers, outlaws, and cowgirls. Descriptions of the lives and contributions of these women on the frontier.

Anderson, J. (1988). *From map to museum: Uncovering mysteries of the past.* New York: Morrow Junior Books.
   This book explains how museum artifacts end up in a museum. It gives an insider's view of how artifacts are located, researched, labeled, and displayed.

Baker, B. (1977). *Settlers and strangers: Native Americans of the desert Southwest and history as they saw it.* New York: Macmillan.
   Rarely is the history of the United States told from the perspective of the Native American. This book is an excellent example of how history can be presented from a different viewpoint. It tells the story of these native dwellers of the Southwest and the encroachment of white civilization.

Blumberg, R. (1987). *The Incredible journey of Lewis and Clark.* New York: Lothrop, Lee & Shepard Books.
   This is an excellent reference book concerning the Lewis and Clark expedition. It takes the entire journey and its participants from the conception of the idea by Thomas Jefferson to the impact of the expedition in later years. Wonderful, detailed museum pieces provide the artwork to support the text.

Brenner, B. (1977). *On the frontier with Mr. Audubon.* New York: Coward. Joseph Mason gets the opportunity of a lifetime; he is asked to accompany John James Audubon on a flatboat down the Mississippi to document new bird and plant species. The text is written in a journal style and is based on a real assistant of Mr. Audubon.

Burt, O. W. (1976). *Ghost towns of the West.* New York: Julian Messner. This book describes five present-day ghost towns. It gives a history of their development and explains why they were not successful.

Collins, J. (1990). *Lawmen of the old west.* New York: Franklin Watts. This book discusses the role of the town marshal, the sheriff, the U.S. marshal, and the Texas Rangers. Along with describing the duties and activities of each of these, the author provides small sketches of representatives of each field. The text is illustrated with old photographs.

Collins, J. (1990). *Exploring the American West.* New York: Franklin Watts. This book provides brief biographies of some famous explorers. Those included are Daniel Boone, Lewis and Clark, Robert Stuart, Jed Smith, Joseph Walker, and John Frémont.

Connell, K. (1993). *These lands are ours: Tecumseh's fight for the old Northwest.* Austin, TX: Steck-Vaughn Co. This book portrays the many sides of Tecumseh: military leader, orator, and politician. It tells of his efforts to unite his Shawnee people with other tribes in an effort to preserve Indian lands.

Conrad, P. (1985). *Prairie songs.* New York: Harper & Row. This is the story of a family living in the Nebraska territory. It provides a good picture of the trials and hardships faced by pioneers. This is best demonstrated by the difficulties faced by a new doctor and his frail wife who move to Nebraska from the East. Although the story has some depressing incidents, the book is basically an uplifting story of survival.

Fleischman, S. (1962). *Mr. Mysterious & Company.* New York: Little. This is a story of a family that traveled throughout the West performing magic shows in small pioneer towns. In this book they are making their final tour and hope to settle in California by Christmas Day. Their adventures include helping to capture an outlaw.

Fox, M. V. (1991). *The story of women who shaped the west.* Chicago: Children's Press. This is part of the *Cornerstones of Freedom* series. The book discusses the contributions of women to the settling and growth of the west.

Freedman, R. (1988). *Buffalo hunt.* New York: Holiday House. This book describes the Indians' relationship with the buffalo of the plains. The author depicts a buffalo hunt and the ways in which the buffalo was used by Indians. The text is accompanied by paintings by George Catlin and Karl Bodmer.

Freedman, R. (1987). *Indian chiefs*. New York: Holiday House.
This book tells the stories of six famous Indian leaders: Red Cloud, Satanta, Quanah Parker, Washakie, Chief Joseph, and Sitting Bull. In an unbiased account the author chronicles the encroachment of whites on Indian lands west of the Mississippi. This provides a balance to the accounts usually presented in texts about Native Americans.

Goble, P. (1984). *Buffalo Woman*. New York: Macmillan.
A brave young hunter falls in love with Buffalo Woman, who is a member of the Buffalo Nation. When his tribe rejects his wife and son and forces them to return to her family, the young hunter follows. He must prove his love for his wife and son by identifying them among the other buffalo.

Gorsline, M., & Gorsline, D. (1978). *Cowboys*. New York: Random House.
This informative book details the lives of cowboys who rode the cattle trails of the West. Descriptions and uses of equipment and clothing are detailed. The book discusses the life on the Chisholm Trail from cattle ranches in Texas to train depots and stockyards in Abilene and Dodge City, Kansas. The illustrations are excellent.

Gregory, K. (1989). *Jenny of the Tetons*. San Diego: Harcourt Brace Jovanovich.
Jenny's family is massacred by Indians who attacked their wagon train. Instead of continuing westward with the survivors of the wagon train or returning East to live with relatives, Jenny agrees to move in with a trapping family to help with chores. Jenny does not realize that the trapper's wife is a Native American; learning about Indian ways helps Jenny to overcome the grief of losing her own family.

Heth, C., (Ed.). (1992). *Native American dance: Ceremonies and social traditions*. Washington, DC: National Museum of the American Indian.
This book discusses Native American dances, their origins, and their contributions to the present-day culture of Native Americans. Dances from a variety of tribes are discussed. The book also includes information about modern Native American dancers such as Maria Tallchief, Evelyn Cisneros, and Rene Highway. The text is accompanied by beautiful color photographs.

Hook, J. (1989). *American Indian warrior chiefs: Tecumseh, Crazy Horse, Chief Joseph, Geronimo*. Dorset, England: Firebird Books.
This book contains a series of biographies about the great American Indian chiefs listed in the title. Their stories are told in an unbiased fashion. Historical photographs accompany the text.

Katz, W. L. (1977). *Black people who made the old West*. New York: Ethrac Publications.
This book is a comprehensive series of short biographies about black contributors to the history of the old West. The book is divided into these sec-

tions: explorers of a new continent; fur traders; early settlers; rushing for gold; wild, bad, and good cowpunchers; and Lawmen, soldiers, and shapers of the frontier.

Landau, E. (1990). *Cowboys*. New York: Franklin Watts.
This book describes cowboy life from roundups to trail drives. It gives examples of how cowboy traditions continue. Western paintings and photographs are used as illustrations.

Lavine, S. A. (1975). *The houses the Indians built*. New York: Dodd, Mead.
This book shows and describes a variety of Native American housing, including tepees, hogans, igloos, and cliff dwellings. It explains how the type of housing is related to region and culture and provides black-and-white photographs.

Lawler, L. (1992). *Addie's long summer*. Mortion Grove, IL: Albert Whitman & Company.
Addie and her family live in the Dakota prairie. During this summer Addie's family is visited by her city cousins. Addie is embarrassed by her home, her clothes, and her lifestyle when she compares it to that of her sophisticated cousins. Mishaps and adventures lead Addie to a new appreciation of her lifestyle on the prairie.

Laycock, G., & Laycock, E. (1980). *How the settlers lived*. New York: David McKay Company.
This is an excellent resource for gaining information about day-to-day activities of those who settled in the West. There is abundant information related to homes, farming, tools, recreation, and clothing.

Miller, R. H. (1991). *Reflections of a black cowboy. Book one: Cowboys*. Englewood Cliffs, NJ: Silver Burdett.
In this nonfiction text, the author tells the story of black cowboys. Among those discussed are "Deadwood Dick," Willie Kennard, Bill Pickett, Cherokee Bill, and Mary Fields.

Miller, R. H. (1991). *Reflections of a black cowboy. Book two: The buffalo soldiers*. Englewood Cliffs, NJ: Silver Burdett.
The second book of this series shares the role of black army soldiers in the old West by chronicling the lives of individual soldiers.

Pelz, R. (1990). *Black heroes of the wild West*. Seattle: Open Hand Publishing.
This book is a good companion to the Miller books or a good substitute if you cannot find the Miller books. The author discusses the contributions of some of the better-known black pioneers as well as information about black settlers who were not famous.

Place, M. T. (1962). *Westward on the Oregon Trail*. New York: American Heritage Publishing Co.
This reference book provides information on the Oregon Trail, the Mormon Trail, and the many types of people who used these trails. The

reader will learn about trappers, missionaries, gold miners, and regular pioneer families. The text is supplemented by drawings and actual pictures. This text would be a good reference book to assist children in writing research reports for this unit.

Rice, J. (1977). *Cowboy alphabet for grown ups and younguns too.* Austin, TX: Shoal Creek Publishers.

This is a humorous look at cowboy life, A to Z. This book would be an excellent resource for vocabulary study and a springboard for other alphabet books written by students.

Simmons, M. (1990). *When six-guns ruled: Outlaw tales of the Southwest.* Santa Fe, NM: Ancient City Press.

This is fun and an interesting resource. The author tells about famous and not so famous outlaws in New Mexico. Resources for this book included old newspapers of the 1800s and government documents.

Time-Life Books. (1974). *Pioneers.* New York: Time-Life Books.

This book is part of a series on the West completed by this publishing firm. It covers a wide variety of topics that are well documented and presented in an encyclopedic style. Pictures, paintings, and documents lend validity to the written text. One of the most interesting sections is on the prairie schooner. It details how a wagon was built and what kinds of goods the pioneers packed in these wagons. This is an excellent resource book for the classroom.

Tunis, E. (1961). *Frontier living.* Cleveland: World Publishing Company. This book is like an encyclopedia of frontier living. It provides information on topics as varied as school on the frontier and clothing of pioneers. It is a treasure trove of information. If you can locate a copy, it is a must for classroom reference.

Turner, A. (1985). *Dakota dugout.* New York: Macmillan.

This picture book very succinctly and accurately portrays life on the frontier. Although the format is simple, the story and vocabulary are not. This could be an example of the type of book fifth graders might want to write themselves.

Warren, B. (1981). *Indians who lived in Texas.* Dallas: Hendrick-Long Publishing Co.

This book presents Native American tribes such as Caddo, Wichita, Jumano, Tonkawa, Kiowa, Comanche, and Apache who are native to Texas. Simple discussions of clothing, dwellings, foods, and hunting are presented.

Wilder, L. I. (1935). *Little house on the prairie.* New York: Harper & Row.

This book from the Little House series describes how the Ingalls family survived on the prairie. Because this book tells the story from the viewpoint of a young girl, students relate to her adventures very readily. Other books in this series should also be available.

Book Sets

The First Americans. (1992). New York: Benford Books.
This series gives the history and customs of various Native American tribes. The text is enhanced by black-and-white and color photographs. Titles in the series include *California Indians, Indians of the Plateau and Great Basin, Indians of the Plains, and Indians of the Southwest.*

Indians of North America. (1989). New York: Chelsea Publishing.
This series of texts tells about forty-eight different tribes and gives history of the tribes from origins, through arrival of the whites, to the present day. These books present historically accurate information and include many photographs.

Sourcebooks of the American West. (1992). Brookfield, CT: Millbrook Press. These texts provide brief, encyclopedic information regarding events, documents, and people involved in the expansion of the United States. Titles in the series include *Exploring the Frontier* about explorers and map makers; *The Conquest of the West* about battles and diplomacy that expanded U.S. boundaries; *Bridging the Continent* about railroads, trails, and telegraph lines; *The Riches of the West* about trappers, miners, ranchers, and farmers; *Native Americans of the West* about Indians of the various regions, and *The Legendary Wild West.*

The Texians and the Texans. San Antonio: Institute of Texan Cultures.
This series of books presents the contributions of a variety of cultures to Texas history. The eighteen books cover such groups as the Germans, the Indians, the Spanish, the French, the Norwegians, and the Czechs. Other states may also have developed a similar set of books.

Magazines

Cobblestone: History Magazine for Young People
May 1980, vol. 1(5): transcontinental railroad

December 1980, vol. 1(12): Willa Cather

August 1981, vol. 2(8): American buffalo and Plains Indians

December 1981, vol. 2(12): Oregon Trail

May 1982, vol. 3(5): gold rush, California

February 1986, vol. 7(2): Laura Ingalls Wilder

May 1990, vol. 11(5): Sante Fe Trail

September 1990, vol. 11(9): Chief Joseph

Planning Web

Figure 3.3 is a web that combines the ideas and concepts listed during the brainstorming activity and the learning goals from a curriculum guide.

trappers
pioneers
outlaws
cowboys
homesteaders
Chinese laborers
lawmen
Native Americans
trail bosses
soldiers
49ers
buffalo soldiers

Bill Cody
Beckworth
Texas Rangers
Lewis and Clark
Jefferson
Black Kettle
Chief Joseph

log cabins
missions
tepees
pueblos
sod houses
forts

wilderness
territories
mountains
plains
Indian Territory
map skills
exploration

courage
survival
hardworking

LIFE WEST OF THE
MISSISSIPPI—1800s

buffalo
ponies
mustangs

square dancing
folk songs
legends
weaving, basketry
museums

stagecoach
railroad
covered wagons
transportation
villages and towns

textbook, globes, maps
Little House on the Prairie
Sourcebooks of the American West
Sarah, Plain and Tall
Legend of the Bluebonnet
Prairie Songs

gold rush
Oregon Trail
Pony Express
Louisiana Purchase
manifest destiny
Little Big Horn
Wounded Knee
treaties

Figure 3.3 Planning web for "Life West of the Mississippi in the 1800s."

UNIT OBJECTIVES

From the planning web, which is a combination of concepts and ideas about pioneer life and the goals mandated by curriculum guidelines, the following objectives are listed. They are divided into knowledge, skill, and attitude objectives.

Knowledge Objectives

The student will learn:

1. Tribes of Native Americans were the first to settle the North American continent, long before whites came from Europe.
2. People who moved away from the established settlements in the original colonies of the United States were called *pioneers*. These people moved west in search of land, wealth, religious tolerance, and adventure.
3. The white settlers and the Native Americans generally had opposing views on the idea of ownership of land. The whites believed in individual ownership of land; Native Americans believed that no one person could own a piece of land.
4. The American government made treaties with individual tribes and chiefs that often forced the Native Americans onto reservations. Treaties were often broken by the government as new demands for land were made by individuals, railroads, or other businesses.
5. Fighting began between the settlers and the Native Americans. Tales of these battles biased white settlers against the Indians.
6. American government representatives negotiated with Napoleon of France for the purchase of French lands in North America. France agreed to sell a large territory west of the Mississippi that became known as the Louisiana Purchase.
7. Meriwether Lewis and William Clark were sent by President Thomas Jefferson to explore lands included in the Louisiana Purchase. They studied, took notes, and drew pictures of the things they saw. They also made initial contacts with the Indians in the area.
8. President Jefferson sent Zebulon Pike to study the land around the Mississippi River and the southern border of the Louisiana Purchase.
9. The settling of the West opened the way for many professions: farmers, trappers, adventurers, carpenters, blacksmiths, teachers, doctors, and lawyers.
10. "Manifest destiny" became the name of the dream of many Americans to settle in the far West.

Continued.

UNIT OBJECTIVES—Cont'd.

11. Many people traveled west in groups, or trains, of covered wagons. The first major trail was the Oregon Trail.

12. Settlers rushed to California when gold was discovered at Sutter's Mill in 1849. These people in search of striking a rich vein of gold were called *49ers*.

13. Life on the frontier was hard and bleak. Harsh weather, violence, and loneliness were constant contributors to the pioneers' hard life.

14. The transcontinental railroad linked the east coast of the United States with the west coast. The western section of this railroad was built in large part by Chinese immigrants and the eastern part was built by Irish immigrants.

Skill Objectives

Students will:

1. Be able to trace routes of famous journeys west, locate key settlement cities, and locate various regions of the United States on a map or globe.

2. Develop writing skills through journals, letters, stories, and reports.

3. Develop construction and problem-solving skills through the construction of a model. Some examples of models that students might choose to create are a pioneer town, a fort, or a Native American village.

4. Locate and gather information through library research.

5. Learn cooperation skills through working together on projects, taking turns, and respecting the ideas and property of their peers.

6. Develop listening skills by listening to the ideas and presentations of others.

7. Learn to read for a purpose as they use the reference and resource materials available to create research reports.

Attitude Objectives

Students will:

1. Develop an appreciation of the courage and tenacity of pioners who helped to expand our country.

2. Learn the importance of the interdependence of people, products, and services to the growth and prosperity of community life.

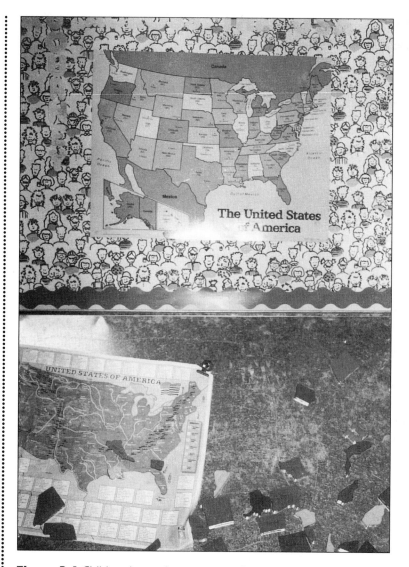

Figure 3.4 Children learn about westward expansion through mapping activities.

3. Develop a respect for the variety of Native American cultures in the United States.

4. Gain an awareness of the variety of cultures and ethnic groups that contributed to the development of the western part of the United States.

ACTIVITIES

The activities for this unit are divided into three groups: initiating activities, developing activities, and concluding activities. The activities are designed to address the goals and objectives for learning and best utilize the resources available. Teachers using this book should feel free to adapt these lists of activities to fit their own similar units. Students should also have input and choice regarding the activities to be completed. The teacher might start with the suggestions here and then modify or delete as necessary.

Initiating Activities

Initiating activities are those designed to activate students' prior knowledge of the topic and to generate interest in the study. They may be activities that are begun in the first few days of the unit but are completed later in the unit.

1. The unit might begin with a K-W-L activity (Ogle, 1986) using information from the basic text. The teacher would start by asking students what they *know* about life west of the Mississippi during the 1800s. This would give the teacher some knowledge about the students' prior knowledge. The second step is what the students *want* to know about the topic. The ideas and questions generated during this portion of the K-W-L might later guide research completed by individual students or small groups. The last part of this activity would require the students to read selected portions of the text to answer their questions. They would then respond with what they had *learned*. The students might want to use the last section as part of a wall chart where they record new and interesting information they locate during their study.

2. Share excerpts from one of the texts on children in the West. Discuss what daily life for a young person would be like. Draw comparisons to their own lives through role playing, art activities, or discussions.

3. Students should have the opportunity to browse through the supplemental texts and self-select a book from the supplemental list to read during free reading time. Create sharing-response groups.

Developing Activities

Developing activities compose the major part of the unit. They should provide students the opportunity to experience a variety of activities through several media. As much as possible, provide opportunities for some whole class work, some small group work, and some individual work. The teacher may initiate some of the activities; however, students should also be encouraged to create their own activities and to choose their own method of presentation. Because student choice and responsibility are so important, the following activities should be presented only as suggestions. In this unit students can:

1. View slides or videos pertaining to the westward movement. They can choose their own method of responding to the information presented.

2. Play *Oregon Trail*, which is a simulation of life in a covered wagon on the trail to settlements in Oregon. Discussion of their experiences could be shared in reports, art, or drama.

Figure 3.5 Computer software is a valuable resource.

Continued.

ACTIVITIES—Cont'd.

3. Choose a particular imaginary character and create a journal for daily entries about life west of the Mississippi. Some suggestions of characters that might be chosen are a pioneer on the trail, a child who lives near a fort on the prairie, a Native American child who is forced to leave because of the encroachment of whites, or a woman who is responsible for creating a home life on the frontier. This journal should be developed throughout the duration of the unit.

4. Conduct research at a local art museum or living history museum.

5. Imagine you are one of the first settlers of a pioneer town or village. Write to friends back east and try to convince them to move to your town. Tell them all of the advantages of such a move.

6. Pretend you are one of the soldiers hired to explore with Lewis and Clark. Your personal bag may weigh only two and a half pounds. Using the word processing program on the computer, write about what you would take and explain your choices.

7. Create a newspaper advertisement to entice people to move west.

8. Create a newspaper for this period. Include news items as well as advertisements.

9. Make a pictorial map of the Lewis and Clark expedition. Include a legend and scale of miles.

10. Locate copies of one or more of the treaties between the American government and a Native American tribe. Compare the promises made within the treaties to what actually occurred.

11. Using a map of the Louisiana Purchase, draw and color the states eventually formed from this territory, or create a map from salt dough or another medium.

12. Write a play about some aspect of pioneer life, Native American life, exploration, mining, or other western topic.

13. Compute the following: (a) How many acres of land did the United States gain in the Louisiana Purchase? (Note: 1 acre = 0.0015625 square miles.) Round your answer to the nearest acre. (b) What was the cost per acre?

14. Construct a model such as a pioneer town, a fort, a Native American village (choose a particular tribe such as Apache, Cheyenne, or Kiowa), or a mode of transportation.

15. Create a mural showing the westward spread of settlers in America.

16. Create paper dolls or puppets to demonstrate the way pioneers, cowboys, Native Americans, or other groups dressed.

17. Learn the steps to a Native American dance and demonstrate or teach it to other students.

18. Make a quilt.

19. Investigate the various beadwork or pottery patterns of several Native American tribes.

20. Present personal writings or readings to others through an author's chair (Graves & Hansen, 1983).

Concluding Activities

Concluding activities help bring closure to the unit. With these activities, the students should demonstrate their knowledge of the concepts of the unit.

1. Have a pioneer day celebration. Have the students dress as different characters from the frontier. They may want to dress as the person for whom they have been writing the journal. Play games and activities that pioneer and Native American children may have played. Foods, or facsimiles, could be served. Have a quilting bee or study from old textbooks such as McGuffey Readers.

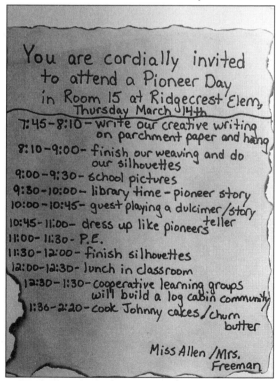

Figure 3.6 Pioneer Day invitation.

Continued.

ACTIVITIES—Cont'd.

2. The students might use the last few days of the unit to share projects, such as the village constructions, with the rest of the class. They could be set up like an exhibition, and classmates and other classes could tour the exhibit.

3. As a whole class or in small groups, return to the original K-W-L activity and add any new information. Use it as a review of the unit concepts.

EVALUATION

The evaluation for any unit should allow for student self-evaluation, for peer evaluation for teacher unit evaluation, and for teacher evaluation of student progress.

Student self-evaluation takes place when students complete specific activities and during the concluding activity in which the students list the concepts they have learned and compare that list with their initial brainstorming list. The comparison activity allows students to assess how much they have learned from the activities and class or group discussions. The teacher might also ask each student to write a paragraph about the most important idea or piece of knowledge learned during the unit.

Students should frequently evaluate peer presentations, group participation, and projects. These evaluations should be constructive in nature and provide the student information related to improving the activity. For example, when a student reads a story or report to a group of students, the audience of students should ask questions and contribute comments that help the student clarify the writing, expand the information, or research new areas of concern. In group work, members of the group should evaluate the performance of the group as well as the performance of each member. Checklists developed by the students or the teacher can facilitate peer evaluation.

The teacher's evaluation of the unit is an ongoing process. As each activity is completed, the teacher should note the following: What was successful about the activity? What was unsuccessful for all the children or for some of the children? What could the teacher have done to be better prepared for the activity? What new ideas occurred that could be used the next time the unit is taught?

The teacher can evaluate the students through their daily work, through their projects, and through written assignments. The teacher will also want to consider the students' evaluation of their own learning and seek the students' input on specific projects. Figures 3.7, 3.8, 3.9, and 3.10 are evaluation tools that the teacher and students can adapt for their own use.

RESEARCH REPORT CHECKLIST
FOR PEER EVALUATION

Student: _____ Title: _____ Date: _____

CONTENT:

_____ Ideas are clearly stated.

_____ Information is accurate.

_____ Writing is in student language (own words).

_____ Stays with the topic.

_____ Avoids repetition of common words; uses synonyms.

_____ Includes illustrations and/or graphics.

STRUCTURE:

_____ Material is accurately divided into paragraphs.

_____ Introduction captures the interest of the reader.

_____ Includes a summary sentence or paragraph.

_____ Sources are acknowledged and listed.

MECHANICS:

_____ Uses correct punctuation.

_____ Capitalizes words appropriately.

_____ Has subject–verb agreement throughout.

_____ Avoids run-on sentences and sentence fragments.

_____ Has correct spelling.

Figure 3.7 Sample checklist for peer evaluation.

Continued.

EVALUATION—Cont'd.

KNOWLEDGE OBJECTIVES CHECKLIST

Student:_____

Objective	Activity	Level of Understanding	Date
#1 Native Americans			
#2 Pioneers			
#3 Ownership of land			
#4 Treaties			
#5 Fighting between Native Americans and settlers			
#6 Louisiana Purchase			
#7 Lewis and Clark			
#8 Pike			
#9 Professions			
#10 Manifest destiny			
#11 Oregon Trail			
#12 Gold rush			
#13 Hard life			
#14 Transcontinental railroad			

Figure 3.8 Knowledge objectives log.

SKILL OBJECTIVES CHECKLIST

Student:_____

Objective	Activity	Level of Understanding	Date
#1 Trace routes			
#2 Writing			
#3 Construction/ problem solving			
#4 Library research			
#5 Cooperation			
#6 Listening			
#7 Reading for a purpose			

Figure 3.9 Skill objectives log.

ATTITUDE OBJECTIVES CHECKLIST

Student:_____

Objective	Activity	Level of Understanding	Date
#1 Appreciation of courage			
#2 Importance of interdependence			
#3 Respect for Native American culture			
#4 Diversity			

Figure 3.10 Attitude objectives log.

Content Activities as a Supplement to Studying a Single Piece of Literature

··

THE ENORMOUS EGG

Model

A second model often used in developing a unit of instruction is the literature–centered model. When choosing this model, the teacher selects a single book for the children to read and enjoy. The teacher looks for opportunities to help children make connections with other content areas they are or will be studying, but the primary emphasis is on the story itself. This model is probably the easiest to prepare because related content, while interesting and important, is only supplemental.

Focus

The focus for this unit is *The Enormous Egg* (1987) by Oliver Butterworth. It is a delightful book to read and a good example of high-quality literature. The book has a clear story line, well-developed characters, and even some suspense.

This unit is planned for fourth-grade students who would have a wonderful time imagining all kinds of potential problems in having to care for a pet like Uncle Beazley. Because most fourth graders have studied a unit on dinosaurs at an earlier grade, they have some background knowledge about dinosaurs and are also able to see the unusual situation created by the discovery of a dinosaur egg in today's world.

The readability level of this book is appropriate for most fourth-grade students, and the book has the potential for making connections with other subject areas. There are, of course, the possibilities for further investigations into the world of dinosaurs in the area of science, a look at the legislative process in the social studies, and even opportunities to integrate math. Primary emphasis here is the area of language arts; therefore, the time set aside for language arts in this classroom is used for reading and sharing *The Enormous Egg*.

The unit is designed for a twelve- to fifteen-day period, but information and ideas presented here could be expanded as student interest or needs dictate.

Brainstorming

After a quick review of the book, a group of fourth-grade teachers gathered to brainstorm potential ideas and activities for the unit. The following ideas were generated from this brainstorming session.

dinosaurs	make a story map
problem solving	character sketches
point of view	write and illustrate
how a bill becomes a law	Washington, D.C.
make a vocabulary dictionary	write a news release
graph growth of dinosaur	prediction activities
make a skeletal model	measure size of triceratops
fact vs. fiction	extinction of dinosaurs—How?
character maps	characterizations—adjectives
hatch a chicken egg	visit museum
write/perform a play	write congressperson
group work	literature response log
enjoyment	

Figure 3.11 Related ideas from brainstorming.

CURRICULUM GUIDES

Because the focus of this unit is a single piece of literature, *The Enormous Egg,* the area of language arts supplies most of the concepts. However, other content areas, particularly science and social studies, are consulted. The goals listed next represent curricular concepts that could be integrated into this unit for fourth graders.

Students will have the opportunity to:

1. Increase their vocabularies
2. Use dictionary and glossary skills
3. Predict outcomes
4. Listen for main ideas
5. Distinguish fact, opinion, and fantasy
6. Use figurative language
7. Learn to use context clues to gain the meaning of unknown words
8. Apply critical and creative thinking skills to literature
9. Become more fluent in giving oral reports

Continued.

CURRICULUM GUIDES—Cont'd.

10. Use correct punctuation, grammar, and capitalization in writing
11. Take notes
12. Solve simple measurement problems
13. Use estimation and approximation
14. Learn more about fossils and rocks
15. Relate art to all areas of the curriculum
16. Cooperate with others on projects in various subject fields
17. Learn about American government
18. Use the newspaper as a resource
19. Write letters.

Resources

In addition to a sufficient number of copies of *The Enormous Egg,* the teacher should gather some supplemental resource books on dinosaurs, some information on Washington, D.C., and some resources to use in studying the process of making laws in our country. It is important to be sure that the resources selected will meet the varying reading levels of students in the classroom. It is also important to include fiction and non-fiction books as resources. The following books can be used in connection with this unit.

Cohen, D., & Cohen, S. (1992). *Where to find dinosaurs today.* New York: Puffin Books.
This nonfiction book is really a state-by-state guide to dinosaur sites and museums. Children could really help their parents plan a "dinosaur hunt" vacation in their own state or across the country based on information provided in this book.

Coy, H. (1965). *The first book of Congress.* New York: Franklin Watts.
This nonfiction book provides simple introduction to the U.S. Congress. Children learn of the House of Representatives and the Senate. The book contains a section "The Story of a Bill," which provides a simple description of the process from the introduction to the president's signature.

Green, C. (1985). *Congress: A new true book.* Chicago: Children's Press.
The functions and interrelationships of the two houses of Congress are described in very simple language. Children can easily read and understand the section "How a Law Is Made."

James, M. (1964). *A young explorer's Washington.* New York: New York Graphics Society.
This unique book takes the reader on a walking tour of many important buildings in and around Washington, D.C. It is filled with simple maps of everything from the White House to the Naval Academy at Annapolis to the Shenandoah National Forest. It is helpful in giving children a perspective of the hundreds of unique places and people in the immediate vicinity of the nation's capital.

Krementz, J. (1987). *A visit to Washington, D.C.* New York: Scholastic.
The reader follows a six-year-old boy on a visit to Washington, D.C. The book contains a very simple text accompanied by photographs. The photographs include buildings of importance like the White House and the Gallery of Art, but also monuments from recent history, such as the Vietnam Memorial.

Miers, E. S. (1965). *The Capitol and our lawmakers.* New York: Charles E. Merrill Books.
This nonfiction book gives children a sense of history as they tour the Capitol. The book contains actual photographs taken at various times in the history of the city. Although this is not a new book, the historical perspective is a valuable one to add to children's knowledge.

Munro, R. (1987). *The inside-outside book of Washington, D.C.* New York: Puffin Books.
The author gives children an unusual tour through Washington, D.C. While visiting monuments and important buildings, they see them from the inside and the outside.

Packard, M. (1981). *Dinosaurs.* New York: Simon and Schuster.
Children are always asking questions about dinosaurs. The author of this book uses a question-and-answer format to provide the reader with factual information about dinosaurs. The text, illustrations, a timeline, and an atlas provide specific facts about different kinds of dinosaurs.

Sasek, M. (1969). *This is Washington, D.C.* New York: Macmillan.
Children are introduced to Washington, D.C., in this nonfiction book. They see Capitol Hill, where bills become laws, in addition to many other fascinating sites. The book contains many accurate drawings that help children "see" the city.

Steiner, B. (1986). *Oliver Dibbs and the dinosaur cause.* New York: Macmillan.
A fifth-grade student, Oliver, tries to get his classmates involved in a project to make the stegosaurus the state fossil for Colorado. Ollie's class works hard to get a bill through the legislature, but the legislature fails to pass it before they recess for the summer. The book's surprise ending should make the reader smile just like Oliver. Children would enjoy finding similarities between this book and *The Enormous Egg.*

Zanini, G. (1983). *The dinosaur book.* New York: Greenwich House, Crown Publishers.
The author traces the development of life on the earth, from single plants and animals to dinosaurs, and then to humans. The chapter "The Great Lizards" provides the reader with specific information about the triceratops and other dinosaurs.

Planning Web

After brainstorming ideas, consulting fourth-grade curriculum guides, and looking for resources, a web similar to the one in Figure 3.12 was created to reflect concepts and connections the teacher and children will make during this unit.

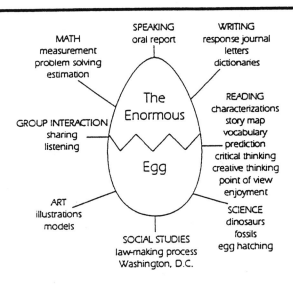

Figure 3.12 Planning web for The Enormous Egg.

UNIT OBJECTIVES

The following unit objectives were developed to provide an outline for the instructional activities of the unit. These objectives are based on the planning web created.

Knowledge Objectives

The students will:

1. Investigate dinosaurs, their habitats, their characteristics, and their extinction
2. Identify parts of a story
3. Identify main characters
4. Learn how a bill becomes a law
5. Learn about interesting places and the history of Washington, D.C.

Process Objectives

The students will:

1. Refine comprehension strategies: making predictions, finding main idea, using context clues, and understanding point of view
2. Increase their vocabulary
3. Practice using the dictionary as they are introduced to new vocabulary
4. Build writing skills through their literature response journals, creative writing, and reports
5. Participate in art activities
6. Measure dinosaurs and compare size (weight and length) with other animals and people
7. Make an oral presentation
8. Improve their abilities to work as members of groups
9. Write a letter using correct form
10. Practice using skills of estimation and approximation

Attitude Objectives

The students will:

1. Enjoy reading this book
2. Have an appreciation for the unique nature of Washington, D.C.
3. Have an appreciation for the workings of our government
4. Value one another's opinions and ideas

ACTIVITIES

The activities for this unit are divided into three groups: initiating activities, developing activities, and concluding activities. The activities are designed to help the teacher and the students meet the goals and objectives for learning and to allow them to engage in an in-depth study of *The Enormous Egg*. Teachers who read this book should feel free to adapt this list of activities to their students' needs and interests.

Initiating Activities

Initiating activities, or introductory activities, for this model are designed primarily to generate student interest and enthusiasm in the book. Although an introduction to *The Enormous Egg* may take place in a single class period, some activities begun in the first few days will not be completed until later in the unit.

1. Create a bulletin board with a large cracked egg at the center. Title for the board could be "What's Inside?" Children should bring pictures from magazines or drawings that illustrate their answers to the question. (This is really a prediction activity.)

2. Establish literature response groups of four or five students who meet daily to make predictions or discuss the chapters read.

3. Create a journal for daily entries about the book. Predictions or purpose-setting questions may be used initially. As the story develops, students may choose a main character and make journal entries from that character's point of view.

4. Make enormous egg dictionaries. Students should record any difficult or unfamiliar words in their personal dictionaries. A class list of vocabulary words is developed from student lists.

5. Read the first chapter of the book to set the stage.

6. Begin a story map with the whole class. Continue building as the story unfolds.

Developing Activities

These activities compose the major part of the unit. Students have an opportunity to experience a variety of activities in individual, small group, and whole class settings. Most activities are required, but often students respond differently to their requirements.

Figure 3.13 *Independent reading is an important aspect of model 2.*

1. Introduce point of view after reading the first chapter. Read *Two Bad Ants* (VanAllsburg, 1988) and *The True Story of the Three Little Pigs* (Scieska, 1989), other examples of point of view. Have small groups rewrite a familiar story from a different point of view.

2. Begin a list of main characters.

3. Create character maps (diagrams), and emphasize descriptive words or actions used by the author.

Continued.

ACTIVITIES—Cont'd.

4. Draw or paint a picture of one of the characters. Your picture should illustrate the words you use in describing the character.

5. Share with members of your group strategies you use to determine the meaning of unknown words.

6. Draw or make a model of a triceratops.

7. Select a different kind of dinosaur, do some research, and prepare to share this information with the class in a short oral report.

8. Make a class game similar to Trivial Pursuit based on information facts gathered about dinosaurs.

9. Set up an incubator and try to hatch chicken or duck eggs. Observe and record observations.

10. Read information books to learn how a bill becomes a law. Make a poster to show the process.

11. Invite your local congressional representative to talk about the law-making process.

12. Watch a movie or filmstrip about Washington, D.C.

13. Visit a museum of natural history or dinosaur exhibition.

14. Graph the weight growth of Uncle Beazley.

15. Measure the length of the dinosaur at various stages of growth. Estimate and then compare these numbers with height of your classmates. (This is a good outdoor activity).

16. Pretend that you are Nate. Write how you would solve the problem of finding food for your pet.

17. Plan a debate in your response group. Choose characters representing the two sides (senators and scientists), and debate Uncle Beazley's fate.

18. Write letters to your senators to persuade them to save Uncle Beazley.

19. With the help of your teacher, think of a project your class could adopt. (Save a historic city building or tree or protect an endangered species.) Plan a media campaign (letters, posters, and more) to present your views. Invite television or radio reporters to hear your presentation.

20. Make a new bulletin board containing drawings and descriptions of characters.

21. Your literature group should create a "Save Uncle Beazley" poster.

22. Have a dinosaur awareness day. Choose a simple fictional book about dinosaurs to read to your kindergarten partner.

Figure 3.14 Students are gathering information for a report on the legislative process.

Concluding Activities

A few culminating or concluding activities help bring closure to the unit. Students should have the opportunity to demonstrate their knowledge and enjoyment through these activities.

1. Prepare and present the play *Little Grunt and the Big Egg* by Tomie dePaola (1990) to kindergarteners and first graders.

2. In your literature group, retell your favorite part of the story. Prepare to read aloud a few pages illustrating your choice.

3. Share your dinosaur report with the class.

4. Play your dinosaur game (modeled after Trivial Pursuit).

EVALUATION

Evaluation of this unit is an ongoing process that reflects students' progress toward unit objectives. Student self-evaluation, teacher evaluation of the unit, and teacher evaluation of student progress are both continuous (formative) and culminating (summative).

Student self-evaluation for this unit begins with a checklist (Figure 3.15). Students check off activities as they complete them. Students demonstrate how much they have learned about characterization through their illustrations and descriptions of characters. They also demonstrate how much they have learned about dinosaurs through their oral reports.

Teacher evaluation of the unit is a daily task. As each activity is completed, the teacher should ask, Was the activity successful? Were all students

Student Activity Checklist for *The Enormous Egg*

Name _____

Daily Activities   **Day Completed**

Individual Activities	1	2	3	4	5	6	7	8	9	10	11	12
Dictionary entries												
Response journal entries												
Character description												
Character illustration												
Dinosaur model												
Oral report												
Measurement activity												
Graphing activity												
Letter writing												
Kindergarten book												
Group projects												
Point of view story												
Uncle Beazley poster												

Figure 3.15 Student activity checklist.

able to participate in the activity? What was not sucessful about this activity? What should I have done differently? What new ideas could I use the next time my class reads the book? How have the children grown? What have I learned about the children through this activity?

The teacher can evaluate students through their daily work, through small group projects, and through the written and oral assignments. Teacher observations of student activities and participation as well as finished pieces of work are used to get a complete picture of student progress and achievements. A sample observation checklist that could be used in evaluating students is presented in Figure 3.16. A checklist such as this one can be designed to document those skills specifically addressed in the unit objectives.

Checklist for Observation

Unit_____

Name_____

Student Activity	Date Observed	Evidence
1. Identifies main idea		
2. Makes predictions		
3. Uses context to identify vocabulary		
4. Uses dictionary in word identification		
5. Identifies point of view		
6. Identifies parts of a story		
7. Uses adjectives to describe characters		
8. Relates story to personal experience		
9. Retells story accurately		
10. Interacts with the text		
11. Reads with expression		
12. Listens to responses of others		
13. Participates in discussions		
14. Orally communicates ideas to group		
15. Uses correct form in writing a letter		

Figure 3.16 Checklist for observation.

Literature and Content as a Balance in the Curriculum

OCEANS: THE WORLD BENEATH THE SEA

Model

This unit is based on model 3, the literature-infused model. Woven into the unit is a collection of children's literature and specific concepts selected from all content areas. Children's tradebooks, fiction and nonfiction, are used as primary sources for the development of concepts and learning activities in this unit. Textbooks and curriculum guides are also examined to assure continuity and legitimacy for the unit of study.

Focus

The focus for this unit is the study of oceans, the world beneath the sea. Children explore real and fanciful concepts, problems, and issues through reading, investigations, and a variety of activities.

The study of water and oceanography is generally included in curriculum guides for second grade. The concepts recommended usually center on earth science and the characteristics or uses of water. Some reference may be made to the impact humans have on the future of the ocean world, but many other possibilities are not included in curriculum guidelines.

Oceans are also addressed in most published second-grade science series. The topic is often part of a larger unit on earth science; therefore, in-depth study of major concepts is not possible. Most texts address the states of water, uses of water, and the location of water on the earth. Some texts devote a few pages to a comparison of salt and fresh water. Some science series introduce the ocean briefly as a habitat for specific plants and animals. Because published science series tend to provide a broad survey of many topics, an in-depth study of oceans is not included.

Using the literature-infused model in planning this unit presents unique opportunities for genuine integration of the concepts included in science and social studies texts with other concepts found in children's tradebooks. Children also explore related concepts such as endangered species, pollution and its effect on the ocean, possible occupations connected with ocean study, and even sunken treasures. Math, language arts, music, and art activities that permit natural integration are included in the unit.

Although curriculum guides and textbooks are consulted, good children's literature is also available to aid in the selection of concepts and learning activities. Specific tradebooks and reference books are chosen to provide the primary sources of information and enjoyment as children investigate the underwater world.

This unit is designed to be used with second graders, but could easily be adapted for use by fifth graders by choosing age-appropriate tradebooks and resources, by planning for more in-depth study of the concepts selected, and by selecting learning activities appropriate for older children.

The unit presented here is designed for four weeks, during which children and teachers have the opportunity to participate in many exciting projects and activities. The unit also provides the setting for children and their teachers to make natural connections between the world of literature and the real world of the ocean.

Brainstorming

The ideas, concepts, and resources presented in Figure 3.17 were the result of a teacher-student brainstorming session. During the brainstorming session, the teacher gains information about students' prior knowledge, misconceptions, and interests.

underwater exploration	scuba diving
plants and animals in the ocean	treasure hunts
endangered species	globe and map skills
shipwrecked	shell collecting
sandpainting	paint a mural of ocean
listen to sound of ocean	visit aquarium
food chains	Ibis
the Titanic	keep journal as ship captain
sunken treasure	historic sailors/captains
Swimmy	whaling
is ocean really blue?	set up aquarium
how big is a whale?	unusual fish
compare ocean creatures—graph	Jacques Cousteau
Humphrey the Lost Whale	taste seafood
write tall tales of "big fish that got away"	map ocean floor
sink and float objects in fresh/salt water	book diaries
occupations	pollution—Exxon Valdez
make sand castles	pirates
The Little Mermaid by Andersen	Popeye, Captain Hook
go on an "ocean cruise"	poems from the sea
submarines	Magic School Bus book

Figure 3.17 Composite of ideas, concepts, and resources from brainstorming.

CURRICULUM GUIDES

The goals listed below were selected from a representative curriculum guide for second grade. Each content area has specific goals which might be utilized in this unit. Students should be provided opportunities to:

Language Arts

Listening
1. Distinguish fact and fancy
2. Distinguish sounds heard in nature
3. Visualize images heard in music
4. Gather facts on field trips

Reading
1. Identify the main idea and supporting details
2. Recognize the difference between fact and opinion
3. Use picture and beginning dictionaries
4. Predict outcomes of stories

Speaking
1. Read and recite poetry
2. Share real and imaginative experiences
3. Use clear and appropriate directions
4. Participate in and contribute to group discussions in a courteous manner

Writing
1. Write a short paragraph, poem, or story
2. Write thank-you notes or friendly letters

Spelling
1. Use correct usage and punctuation in writing and speaking

Math
1. Use > and < symbols
2. Measure and estimate distance
3. Compare length and size
4. Formulate and solve story problems by using addition and subtraction
5. Construct and interpret simple line graphs, bar graphs, or pictographs

Social Studies

1. Use map and globe skills
2. Discuss current events
3. Read graphs and interpret data

Science

1. Investigate the interdependence of plants and animals
2. Identify and compare three states of water
3. Study uses of water and its importance to humans
4. Study water pollution and its effects
5. Study earth's surface (percent covered by water)
6. Learn about animals that live in oceans
7. See how plants and animals adapt to their environment
8. Learn about endangered or extinct species

Music

1. Sing songs
2. Dramatize songs and stories

Art

1. Draw, paint, and sculpt with a wide variety of materials
2. Relate art to all curriculum areas

Physical Education and Health

1. Participate in group play
2. Identify a healthy and safe environment

Resources

The resources listed below were selected for possible use in the study of oceans.

Tradebooks

A House for a Hermit Crab—Eric Carle

Little Whale—Ann McGovern

The Animals Who Changed Their Colors—Pascale Allamand

Kermit the Hermit—Bill Peet

National Geographic Books for Young Explorers
  Exploring the Seashore

Animals That Live in the Sea
The Wonderful World of Seals and Whales
The Fish Who Could Wish—John Bush and Korky Paul
Ibis: The True Whale Story—John Himmelman
Is This a House for a Hermit Crab?—Megan McDonald
Keep the Lights Burning, Abbie—Peter and Connie Roop
Hide and Seek Fog—Alvin Tresselt
The Crab That Played with the Sea (Just So Stories)—Rudyard Kipling
Swimmy—Leo Lionni
The Magic School Bus on the Ocean Floor—Joanna Cole
Oceans—Seymour Simon
The Little Island—Golden MacDonald and Leonard Weisgard
Explorer Books: Sharks—Della Rowland
The Little Mermaid—Hans Christian Andersen
A Jellyfish Is Not a Fish—John Waters
Fish Eyes—Lois Ehlert
Whales: The Gentle Giant—Joyce Milton
Dolphins—June Behrens
Seashores: Nature Club Series—Joyce Pope
Fish Is Fish—Leo Lionni
My Very Own Octopus—Bernard Most
The Sea and I—Harutaka Nakawatari
The Ocean Alphabet Book—Jerry Pallotta
Humphrey, the Lost Whale (A True Story)—Wendy Tokuda and Richard Hall
Sea Squares—Joy N. Hulme
I Am the Ocean—Suzanna Marshak
Big Al—Andrew Clements Yoshi
The Titanic: Lost . . . and Found—Judy Donnelly
Sunken Treasure—Gail Gibbons
Why the Tides Ebb and Flow—Joan Chase Bowden
Under the Sea from A to Z—Anne and Donald Doubilet
The Whale's Song—Dyan Sheldon
Dolphin Adventure—Wayne Grover
Window on the Deep: The Adventures of the Underwater Explorer Sylvia Earle—
    Andrea Conley
My Friend Whale—James Simon

Island Boy—Barbara Cooney

Sam the Sea Cow—F. Jacobs

The Young Scientist Investigates Sea and Seashore—Terry Jennings

Stringbean's Trip to the Shining Sea—Vera B. Williams

A Day Underwater—Deborah Kovacs

Seabird—Clancy Holling

Thy Friend Obadiah—Britton Turkle

The Underwater Alphabet—Jerry Pallotta

Going Lobstering—Jerry Pallotta and Rob Bolster

Poetry

A Child's Treasury of Seaside Verse—Dial Books

The Sea Is Calling Me—Lee Bennett Hopkins

Sea Gifts—George Shannon

The Hopeful Trout and Other Limericks—John Ciardi

Magazines

National Geographic World

Zoobooks

Ranger Rick

Naturescope

Dolphin Log

Computer Software

Voyage of the Mimi

Life in the Oceans

Videos

Animals of a Living Reef—Coronet Films

The Restless Sea—Coronet Films

Other Resources

Center for Marine Conservation

Coastal Awareness Resource Guide

Project Wild

Ocean Related Curriculm Activities (ORCA)

Planning Web

Because the literature-infused model is the most complicated of the three models, creating a web is vital to ensure natural and legitimate connections in the time frame established. The web that follows (Figure 3.18) contains a carefully selected set of concepts and ideas obtained from the brainstorming activity, a limited number of goals chosen from the curriculum guides, and appropriate children's literature selected to serve as primary resources for this unit.

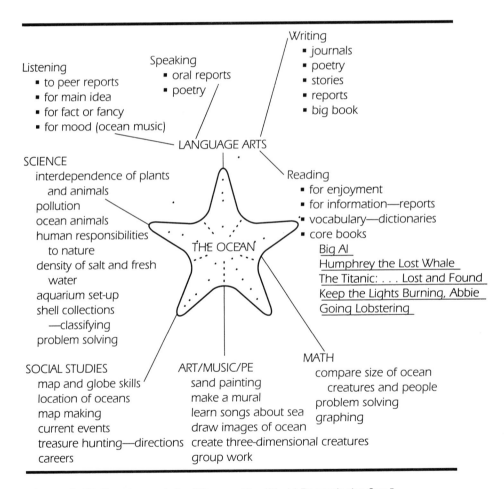

Figure 3.18 Planning web for "Oceans: The World Beneath the Sea."

UNIT OBJECTIVES

From the web, which illustrates connections among subject area concepts and literature, the following objectives have been identified. They are divided into knowledge, process, and attitude objectives.

Knowledge Objectives

The students will:

1. Learn the names and locations of the oceans
2. Be able to describe characteristics of the ocean
3. Identify plants and animals that live in the ocean
4. Discover how plants and animals that live in the ocean have adapted to their habitat
5. Investigate the complex relationships and interdependence of plants and animals in the ocean (e.g., food chains)
6. Investigate the results of upsetting the balance in the ocean and surrounding beaches (plastic pollutants, oil spills, or other pollution)
7. Learn which ocean animals are endangered species
8. Learn about careers associated with oceans (e.g., sailors, divers, marine biologists)
9. Study the variability of depth of the ocean floor
10. Tell how scientists measure the ocean depths
11. Learn about the ways people use the ocean
12. Distinguish fact and fancy about the ocean

Process Objectives

The students will:

1. Read fiction and nonfiction tradebooks and resources for enjoyment and for information
2. Build writing skills through the development of journals, book diaries, reports, stories, and poetry
3. Use beginning research skills as they gather information for oral and/or written reports
4. Develop listening skills as they listen to reports and ideas of others

UNIT OBJECTIVES—Cont'd.

5. Learn cooperation skills such as taking turns, respecting the ideas of others, and sharing materials as they work together on problem-solving activities and creative projects

6. Learn to use prediction strategies as they read

7. Learn to use the newspaper as a resource

8. Use art and music to express their ideas and feelings about the ocean

9. Sharpen their observation and sorting skills as they build a shell collection

Attitude Objectives

The students will:

1. Develop an appreciation for the ocean and the delicate balance surrounding its creatures

2. Enjoy the beauty found in and near the ocean

3. Realize that people have a responsibility to care for the ocean environment and to preserve it for the future

4. Imagine how the ocean might benefit people in the future

Resources

A list of potential resources was identified earlier in the process of building this unit. After the planning web was completed and the unit's goals and objectives were defined, a final list of resources was chosen. The first list contains some books which will be read by the teacher and some that will be part of class sets that will be read by all children. The list also contains many other books that will be used as resources for individual or small group projects. Although the list is quite extensive, numerous others can be found. Each teacher should feel free to select additional materials or to delete those that are not available or do not meet the interests and abilities of the students.

Most commercial science texts for second grade include a chapter or unit about oceanography or water that could be consulted, along with the trade-books suggested. For this particular unit, *Science* by George G. Mallenson et al. (Silver Burdett and Ginn, 1989) and *Discover Science* by Michael R. Cohen et al. (Scott Foresman and Company, 1989) were consulted to verify the appropriateness of this unit for second graders. Teachers should be cautioned, however, that this is not a "science" unit; the literature-infused model used for this unit is much more comprehensive.

Other resources for a unit on oceans might include *National Geographic World Magazine, Zoobooks* (Sharks, Whales), or *Ranger Rick.* A computer simulation game called *Voyage of the Mimi* (Sunburst Co. Wings for Learning) has a number of videos and software involving math, science, geography, and reading. The programs on navigation and whales are most appropriate. Teachers who live in an area that has an aquarium should plan a visit to allow students to see live ocean animals and plants in a habitat much like that of the ocean.

The final list of books chosen follows. Those books selected as core books (to be read by the teacher or class sets) are identified by an asterisk. Both narrative and expository books are included. A variety of reading levels and interests have been considered in the selection. A few books have early publication dates; however, most are quite recent. Also, lists of books contained in issues of *The Reading Teacher* offer even more possible resources.

Core Books

- Class sets

    Keep the Lights Burning, Abbie

    Big Al

    Humphrey the Lost Whale

    The Titantic: Lost. . . and Found

    Going Lobstering

- Teacher read

    The Magic School Bus on the Ocean Floor

    Kermit the Hermit

    Why the Tides Ebb and Flow

    Window on the Deep: The Adventures of Underwater Explorer Sylvia Earle

    The Little Mermaid

    Sea Squares

    I Am the Ocean

    Sunken Treasure

    The Hopeful Trout and Other Limericks

Final Resource List

Amos, W. H. (1984). *Exploring the seashore.* Washington, DC: National Geographic Society.

Children will delight in all of the wonderful creatures found along the seashore. This Book for Young Explorers is another of *National Geographic's* exceptional books for young children. Photographs and paintings are used to invite children to walk along the beach.

*Bowden, J. C. (1979). *Why the tides ebb and flow*. Boston: Houghton Mifflin Co.
This is an enchanting folktale that attempts to explain why the ocean has tides. The wonderful illustrations of Marc Brown carry the reader along to an unexpected ending. This book, along with others, could introduce children to the use of "just-so" stories to explain nature's actions.

Carle, E. (1988). *A house for hermit crab*. Jefferson City, MO: Scholastic.
This is a wonderful story about the travels of a hermit crab. Children will learn about real ocean creatures as the hermit crab travels along the ocean floor looking for a home. Once again, Eric Carle's illustrations capture the imagination of his readers.

*Ciardi, J. (1989). *The hopeful trout and other limericks*. New York: Houghton Mifflin.
Ciardi's magic is shared in limericks that are fun to read. The book also gives children a wonderful model to use in writing limericks.

*Clements, A. (1988). *Big Al*. New York: Scholastic.
Big Al is a big, scary-looking fish who had no friends. Even though he was very friendly, no one trusted him because he had big eyes and big teeth. Al's rescue of a whole school of fish earns him new respect and many friends. The illustrations help tell a touching story of friendship.

*Cole, J. (1992). *The magic school bus on the ocean floor*. New York: Scholastic.
This book is the latest in the *Magic School Bus* series. Miss Frizzle's class takes a field trip on their "not-so-ordinary" schoolbus. A simple trip to the beach becomes an undersea adventure as the bus goes right into the ocean. Children are introduced to plants and animals that live in the ocean, the continental shelf, a coral reef, and even a hot vent. The book provides a wonderful combination of fact and fancy.

*Conley, A. (1991). *Window on the deep: The adventures of the underwater explorer Sylvia Earle*. New York: Franklin Watts.
This book gives children a wonderful look at ocean life and scuba diving. The photographs and beautiful illustrations are sure to capture children's imagination as they are introduced to a real, live scuba diver.

Cooney, B. (1988). *Island boy*. New York: Trumpet.
The story of Matthais Tibbett is a wonderful family story. The independence and self-reliance of this boy's life are central to this touching story. Although it is not specifically about the ocean, Matthais's spirit is representative of many who live or work near the sea.

Crow, S. L. (1984). *The wonderful world of seals and whales*. Washington, DC: National Geographic Society.

Underwater photographs and paintings take children into the world of whales and seals. Children will find new information in both the photographs and the text. This Book for Young Explorers brings children closer to understanding some of the mysteries of these beautiful animals.

Darling, K. (1991). *Manatees on location*. New York: Lothrop, Lee and Shepard Books.

This is an excellent information book on the manatee, a marine mammal. The author provides information on the anatomy of the manatee, their six senses, and their relationship with humans. These topics and others are accompanied by wonderful photographs taken by the author's daughter, Tara.

Darling, K. (1991). *Walrus on location*. New York: Lothrop, Lee and Shepard Books.

Kathy and Tara Darling, a mother-and-daughter team, traveled to Alaska to photograph and document walruses in their natural habitat. The result is a book filled with interesting facts and intriguing photos.

Davies, E. (1980). *Ocean frontiers*. New York: Viking.

This information text discusses how scientists explore the depths of the oceans. Descriptions and explanations are given for such tools as submarines, submersibles, and periscopes. Instructions are given for making some of the tools and for conducting related experiments. This is an excellent reference book.

*Donnelly, J. (1987). *The Titanic: Lost . . . and found*. New York: Random House.

This Step into Reading book was written for second- and third-grade readers. It is a nonfiction book containing an account of the maiden voyage of the *Titanic*. The authors describe the beauty and unique features of this large ship, the crash into the iceberg, the reactions of the people to the disaster, and the final disappearance of the ship. Children are also introduced to scientist Robert Ballard's discovery of the sunken *Titanic* and his commitment to preserve the peace of the wonderful ship.

Doubilet, A., & Doubilet, D. (1991). *Under the sea from a to z*. New York: Crown.

David Doubilet provides children a photographic introduction to life under the sea. This beautiful book also contains fascinating information about each picture. It would be a good resource for written or oral reports.

*Gibbons, G. (1988). *Sunken treasure*. New York: Harper Collins.

This is an informative Reading Rainbow book about the exciting world of treasure hunting. The author gives an interesting account of an underwater treasure hunt by introducing each phase in the operation from the sinking to the search, the eventual find, and the salvage of treasure. The language is simple, and the illustrations make treasure hunting come alive.

Grover, W. (1990). *Dolphin adventure: A true story.* New York: Greenwillow.
Grover shares a real-life adventure for children to enjoy. His personal encounter with three dolphins and his rescue of the baby dolphin are a good introduction to the danger some marine animals face from fishers. The story touches adults as well as children.

Heller, R. (1992). *How to hide an octopus and other sea creatures.* New York: Platt and Munk Publishing.
Realistic illustrations and a beautifully rhymed text tell how ocean creatures use camouflage to protect themselves. The book gives the reader an introduction into some very unusual and beautiful sea creatures.

Hopkins, L. B. (1986). *The sea is calling me.* New York: Harcourt Brace Jovanovich.
The book contains a collection of poems by a number of authors, each poem sharing a brief glance at the ocean, seashells, sandcastles, or other objects associated with the sea. The illustrations help to create a feeling of peace, sand, and nature for the reader. This might be a good book to use as a model for children's poetry writing.

*Hulme, J. N. (1991). *Sea squares.* New York: Hyperion Books for Children.
The author's playful rhymes have children counting sea animals like clown fish, seals, and squids. In a unique fashion, children square numbers from one to ten. Carol Schwartz's beautifully framed illustrations give the text a special touch. The book is great for introducing math concepts related to multiplication.

James, S. (1991). *My friend whale.* New York: Bantam.
This book tells a delightful story about a little boy's friendship with a blue whale. Simple words and wonderful pictures also provide children with information about whales and the delicate balance in their environment.

Kipling, R. (1952). The crab that played with the sea. In *Just So Stories.* New York: Doubleday.
Children are introduced to the rise and fall of the tides through the mischievous adventures of Pau Amma the Crab. They should be led to explore the real reasons for this or other similar natural occurrences.

Kovacs, D. (1987). *A day under water.* New York: Scholastic.
Alvin, a special submarine designed to descend into the ocean to 13,000 feet, was equipped to help scientists study the ocean. By using actual

photographs taken by Alvin, the authors explore the ocean floor through the eyes of three scientists inside the submarine.

Lionni, L. (1968). *Swimmy*. New York: Pantheon Books.
This well-known book tells the wonderful story of one tiny fish named Swimmy and his brothers and sisters. Children are introduced to the concept of food chains, as Swimmy and his family encounter a large tuna. Their creative, imaginative escape plan gives children an unusual twist and a happy ending to the story.

*Marshak, S. (1991). *I am the ocean*. New York: Little, Brown.
The ocean sings a song of its beauty and all the creatures that live in it. The book reads easily and in a lyrical manner, inviting children to sing along. The illustrations of James Endicott capture the beauty of ocean creatures, from the tiniest shell to the giant whale.

McDonald, G., & Weisgard, L. (1946). *The little island*. New York: Scholastic.
No study of the ocean would be complete without reading this classic Caldecott Award book. The small kitten's visit to the island is just a part of the magic of this story. Children hear and feel the rhythm of the sea that surrounds this little island.

McGovern, A. (1979). *Little whale*. New York: Four Winds Press.
This is a factual story of a baby humpback whale. The book contains information about characteristics and habits of this kind of whale told in narrative form. The book also introduces children to whale hunters and their threat to the survival of these magnificent creatures.

Milton, J. (1989). *Whales, the gentle giants*. New York: Random House.
This is a simple Step into Reading book written for beginning readers. It is a nonfiction book that introduces children to some of the different kinds of whales, their characteristics, and their habits. It could be a good resource for report writing.

Most, B. (1980). *My very own octopus*. New York: Harcourt Brace Jovanovich.
This is a wonderfully told story of a little boy who imagines that he has an octopus for a pet. The special characteristics of the octopus make it a lovable and unusual pet. This is a just-for-fun book that also gives children an opportunity to talk about real and imaginary.

Nakawatari, H. (1990). *The sea and I*. New York: Farrar, Straus, and Giroux.
This exquisitely illustrated picture book, told from the perspective of a young Japanese boy, reveals a special reverence for the sea. Although the boy and his father, a fisherman, never appear in the illustrations, the reader senses their love and respect for one another and the sea. The color and beauty of the illustrations make this an award-winning book that must be used.

Pallotta, J. (1986). *The ocean alphabet book.* Watertown, MA: Charlesbridge.
Jerry Pallotta and illustrator Frank Mozzola take children on an alphabetical journey through the North Atlantic Ocean. Children are introduced to unusual and fascinating details about creatures that live in the sea.

Pallotta, J. (1990). *Going lobstering.* Watertown, MA: Charlesbridge.
Two young children are taken on their first search for lobsters. Realistic illustrations and accurate information about lobsters make the reader feel that they, too, are riding on the Lobstertail in search of those creatures with snapping claws. This is a good book to use when talking about careers depending on the ocean.

*Peet, B. (1965). *Kermit the hermit.* Boston: Houghton Mifflin.
Kermit is a grumpy, greedy hermit crab who lives all alone. He finds his life suddenly changed when a young boy rescues him from a sandy grave. The author weaves a wonderful story of gratitude as Kermit tries to find a way to repay his rescuer.

Pope, J. (1990). *Seashores.* Mahwah, NJ: Troll Associates.
The book provides a description of a variety of interesting animals that live in or near the ocean. This Nature Club book contains good illustrations and would be a good reference source to assist children in writing their reports.

Roop, P., & Roop, C. (1985). *Keep the lights burning, Abbie.* Minneapolis: Carolrhoda Books.
This historical biography tells the story of a brave young girl who lived in a lighthouse in Maine in 1856. During a terrible winter storm off the coast of Maine, Abbie Burgess, daughter of the lighthouse keeper, must single-handedly keep the lights burning to protect the ships at sea. This is an exciting beginning-to-read book in the Reading Rainbow group.

Rowland, D. (1990). *Explorer books: Sharks.* New York: Trumpet.
This reference book, one of the Explorer Books series, provides fascinating facts about sharks. It includes the anatomy of a shark, legends about sharks, and the eating habits of sharks, among other topics. The text includes a few black-and-white pictures.

Rowland, D. (1991). *Explorer books: Whales and dolphins.* New York: Trumpet.
Another of the Explorer Books series, this text offers information about several types of whales. The author includes dolphins as examples of the smallest whales. The text is accompanied by black-and-white photographs.

Sabin, F. (1985). *Oceans.* Mahwah, NJ: Troll Associates.
This book provides basic information about the location and development of the earth's oceans. It briefly mentions the role oceans played in history

and the uses of oceans today. This would be a good supplement to the introduction of a unit on oceans.

Sheldon, D. (1990). *The whale's song.* New York: Dial.
Children are inspired by the beautiful illustrations of this book. It provides an excellent introduction to a study of whales, the sea's magnificent mammals.

Simons, J., & Simons, S. (1991). *Why dolphins call: A story of Dionysus.* New York: Silver Burdett.
This book recounts the Greek legend of Dionysus, son of Zeus. Dionysus, who was sent to earth to show humans how to grow grapes and make wine, is captured by pirates. As punishment the pirates are forced to remain in the sea as dolphins. Their calls to one another would serve as guides to lost sailors.

Straker, J. A. (1978). *Animals that live in the sea.* Washington, DC: National Geographic Society.
This beautifully illustrated book is filled with inviting photographs and simple information about unusual ocean animals. The quality of photographs makes this Book for Young Explorers a real treat for children and their teachers.

*Tokuda, W., & Hall, R. (1986). *Humphrey the lost whale: A true story.* Union City, CA: Heian International.
This true story about Humphrey, a lost humpback whale, grew out of an incident that occurred in the San Francisco Bay area when the authors were working at television stations in California. Children read about Humphrey's struggles as he tried to find his way out of the shallow waters of San Francisco Bay and back to the Pacific Ocean. It is a touching story that makes the reader feel good about Humphrey and his rescuers and, at the same time, learn interesting facts about these creatures and their habits.

Tresselt, A. (1965). *Hide and seek fog.* New York: Mulberry Books.
This beautifully illustrated book reveals both the eeriness and the magic of fog. As villagers in a seaside town cope with the worst fog in twenty years, fishermen and beachcombers return to their homes and wait impatiently to return to work. Children, however, discover the magic of playing hide and seek in the fog. This Caldecott honor book gives children a wonderful vision of life along the seacoast.

Waricha, J. (1991). *Treasure.* New York: Trumpet.
This book describes many different kinds of treasures found in the oceans and the people who hunt for the treasure. Along the topics are the *Atocha,* the *Titanic,* treasures of myth, and treasures of war.

ACTIVITIES

The activities for this unit are divided into three groups: initiating activities, developing activities, and concluding activities. The activities are based on the objectives for learning and provide a natural integration of all content areas and children's literature. Teachers using this book are encouraged to adapt this list of activities to their particular classroom needs and interests. The students choose their own reading partners. The teacher guides students as they organize their working groups for some projects. Grouping strategies used during this unit vary to include interest groups, skill groups, and project groups.

Initiating Activities

Initiating activities should be carefully selected. These activities are designed to generate interest in the unit of study and to activate students' prior knowledge. Some of the activities included in the introduction to the unit of study are continued throughout the four weeks and completed later in the unit.

1. Play a tape of "ocean sounds" (*Solitudes - Seascapes,* vol. 9, Toronto: Dan Gibson Productions Ltd.) as the teacher reads *I Am the Ocean* by Suzanna Marshak. After enjoying the story and the beautiful illustrations, the teacher should ask the students what they know about oceans. Write down all of the student comments on a chart labeled "What do I know about oceans?" When the children have finished sharing what they know, help them group their ideas into categories. This helps them as they address the next question: "What do I want to find out about oceans?" Again, the teacher should record their ideas on chart paper. The questions generated are used for whole class study or for individual and small group projects. Be sure to make the tape of ocean sounds available at a listening station or a learning center.

2. Put up a background for a bulletin board. Children draw or paint pictures of ocean plants and animals they meet in their reading and class activities.

3. Create a journal for daily entries about the "world beneath the sea." Some days the teacher gives suggestions for journal entries: (a) Pretend you are a hermit crab. What kind of home would you look for? (b) How would it feel to swim with the dolphins? (c) Keep a three-day journal as if you were a ship's captain. On other days, journal entries will be children's choice. The journal should be developed throughout the entire unit.

4. Introduce children to the collection of books available in your class-room. Share your expectations for reading these books and tell children how to keep a book diary to record those they read. The teacher should plan to meet with each child to set individual goals for the number of books to be read. Individual differences should be considered. Models for individual student activity sheets are included at the end of the unit plan.

5. Have the children choose a book from the class collection to read during free time. They should plan to share these selections with their reading partner. These could be included in their book diaries.

Figure 3.19 Partners listen to a story from the classroom collection.

Continued.

ACTIVITIES—Cont'd.

6. Begin a word bank of ocean-related words. Words should be added to the word bank daily, based on any whole class or small group activities. The teacher should also encourage children to write down any new or interesting vocabulary words encountered during personal reading. The words they choose could be added to the class word bank or to each child's personal ocean "dictionary."

7. Together students and teacher set up working groups with four or five students in each group. These groups meet for problem solving in math or science, for art, and for some language arts activities including reading and discussing books in class sets. Have each group choose a name for themselves. They will regularly evaluate their group's ability to work together. The teacher will also monitor this.

Developing Activities

Developing activities compose the major part of the unit. They should provide students with a variety of activities from all content areas. The teacher should provide opportunities for whole class activities, some small group projects, and some individual work. Some of these activities may be required, but students should also be given the opportunity to make choices among other activities.

1. Read *The Magic School Bus on the Ocean Floor* and other core books to the whole class. Identify concepts or ideas found in these books that are related to the stated objectives.

2. Groups of four or five students read from "class sets" of books and meet daily for discussion and planned activities. Reading strategy lessons or concept instruction comes from these group meetings.

3. Watch at least one Jacques Cousteau movie or video about the ocean and its inhabitants. The teacher may teach a **minilesson** on ocean inhabitants following the video.

4. Read limericks like *The Hopeful Trout* by John Ciardi. Children then write their own limericks.

5. Introduce children to "just-so stories" like *Why the Tides Ebb and Flow* and "The Crab That Played with the Sea." Discuss role of folktales in explaining nature; compare fact and fancy. They can then write their own "just-so" stories, such as "Why the Starfish Has Five Fingers" or "How the Eel Got Its Electricity."

6. On a map and globe, locate and name the oceans of the earth. Review directions north, south, east, and west as students move from one ocean to another.

7. Using the Magic School Bus book as a reference point, talk about the ocean floor. Introduce pictures from encyclopedias or other resources to help students visualize the ocean floor. Using large graph paper, the teacher and students map the land under the sea to show peaks, valleys, continental shelf, and the like. A similar uneven surface could be put on a bulletin board that children are planning. Graph paper and information about varying depths could be placed at learning center; children might choose to try this activity on their own or with a buddy from an older class.

8. Make a shell collection. Teacher and children may all contribute shells from their personal collections. Shells also provide good opportunities for children to sharpen observation skills, use descriptive words (adjectives), and classify according to similar characteristics. Groups of four or five can come up with their own classification systems for shells and present it to their peers. Shells can also be used for math manipulatives.

9. Take a field trip to a nearby aquarium.

10. Set up an "aquarium room" in an empty classroom or a little-used area in the school. Fill it with three-dimensional creatures, ocean plants, sunken treasures, and other underwater items the children learned about in their reading or viewing.

11. Sample shrimp or crab meat. Enlist parents to contribute these and other foods from the sea. The teacher should send a letter home to parents seeking information about possible food allergies or allergic reactions to seafood.

12. Bring in an experienced scuba diver to tell about the equipment he or she uses in diving. Have the diver share personal experiences about diving. Be sure to read Andrea Conley's book about underwater explorer Sylvia Earle at this time.

13. Use computer to go on the *Voyage of the Mimi,* tracking whales and navigating the ocean.

14. Compare the sizes of various ocean animals. Make a bar graph to show differences in length.

15. Have children measure distances to show the typical length of ocean animals (whale, shark, octopus, etc.). Determine how much longer or shorter some ocean animals are than the students. Ask, "How many children lined up head to toe does it take to be just as long as a blue whale?"

Continued.

ACTIVITIES—Cont'd.

16. Read *Humphrey the Lost Whale.* Trace his journey from the ocean into San Francisco Bay and back to the Pacific Ocean. Bring in newspaper clippings to show this is a true story. Newspaper articles about beached whales would also be useful.

17. Adopt a whale (Whale Adoption Project, International Wildlife Coalition: 1-508-546-9980).

Figure 3.20 Computers allow children to simulate ocean travel.

18. With the help of an aquarium shop owner or tropical fish hobbyist, set up an aquarium in the classroom. Children should assume responsibility for feeding aquarium inhabitants and cleaning the aquarium as needed.

19. Read Wayne Grover's true story about his encounter with dolphins. It can be a starting point for discussions about the danger posed to dolphins and other creatures by fishers and careless tourists. Have established groups of four or five make posters to inform people about such dangers to sea animals. This story might be used to introduce the problem of pollution. If so, bring newspaper articles to show examples.

20. Have children do individual reading for information and write a report about an ocean animal of their choice. The teacher may plan to teach minilessons on selecting good library resources for beginning research assignments.

21. Complete the bulletin board by having children draw or paint ocean animals living at various depths in the ocean.

22. Have children investigate differences in density between fresh water and salt water. Provide children with objects; have them predict whether objects will sink or float, first in fresh water. Record their predictions and findings. Then make predictions about some objects' ability to sink or float in different densities of salt water. Record findings and then compare. The teacher should provide each group with a sheet to use in recording predictions and findings.

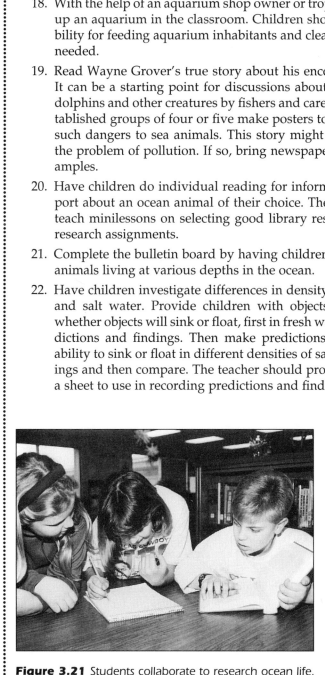

Figure 3.21 Students collaborate to research ocean life.

Continued.

ACTIVITIES—Cont'd.

23. Watch *The Little Mermaid* by Hans Christian Andersen on video. Children may choose to act out parts of the story. Be sure to have multiple copies of different versions of this story available in the classroom.

24. Read *Sunken Treasure* as introduction to scientists who search for treasure under the sea. Perhaps the children can watch a video showing a treasure hunt; Discovery Channel has programs available.

25. Read and write cinquains about the ocean or about animals in the ocean. Teachers may want to present a minilesson and share cinquains they have written.

26. Write poems in the shape of sea animals.

27. Build sand castles, either on sand tables or outside.

28. Build a large submarine or ocean liner of heavy cardboard. Have each working group plot an imaginary trip. They should be prepared to tell their peers about places they would visit and things they might see.

29. Make a sand painting. Ask the art teacher for materials or help.

30. Sing songs about the sea. Examples might be "Humphrey the Whale Song" to the tune of "The Muffin Man" or "Down by the Ocean" by Virginia Stephen. Enlist the help of the music teacher to find or teach songs about the ocean.

31. Make fish mobiles.

32. Have children paint colorful imaginary fish. Cut it out and trace around it. Paint the copy like the front and cut it out. Staple the two fish together around the edges, and stuff the resulting fish with tissue paper. Put it in the aquarium room.

33. Make a large food web on a bulletin board or wall. Show the interdependence of ocean plants and animals.

34. Have children interview a parent or grandparent about fishing experiences. Perhaps have them ask about "the one that got away." Children can record responses obtained during their interviews and share their stories with their peers.

35. Write thank-you notes to guest speakers who came to the class. A brief review on writing thank-you notes or letters may be needed.

Concluding Activities

Concluding activities bring closure to a unit of study. They provide opportunities for children to reflect, make connections, and demonstrate knowledge they have gained during the unit. They will allow children to demonstrate their abilities to collaborate with one another and with the teacher.

1. Make a class big book. Each child should contribute a page containing some new information or ideas. The teacher may limit the topic to *Animals of the Ocean* or choose to have a more inclusive title such as *An Underwater Journey.*

2. Have a treasure hunt, just for fun. Give children a map; each working group could have a different map or set of clues. All students, however, should find the treasure! Treasure hunt could be followed by a "picnic on the beach." (The meal should contain items from the sea such as tuna fish sandwiches). Have parents help with the picnic.

3. Share individual reports about an ocean animal with classmates.

4. Plan a simple program for the parents. Have children write invitations. The program gives children an opportunity to share poems, songs, stories, and/or art they have completed. Each child shares something she or he believes is the best or favorite part of this unit. The music teacher could help lead children in singing songs learned during music class. Be sure to have parents tour the aquarium room.

EVALUATION

Evaluation for a literature-infused unit should be composed of the same three elements as any unit: student self-evaluation, teacher evaluation of student progress, and teacher evaluation of the unit itself. It is important to be sure that the evaluation reflects what was taught and measures students' progress toward unit objectives.

Student self-evaluation for this unit will take a variety of formats.

1. Students are given a checklist to assess their skills in working as members of a small group (Figure 3.22). They are also asked to comment on the effectiveness of their group as a whole. This form of evaluation should be completed at the close of each small group activity.

2. In small group conferences, the children share ideas and concepts they have learned as a result of this unit's activities and discussions. The teacher should meet with each group and record student comments on a chart titled "What did I learn about the ocean?" In comparing this list with the original brainstorming list, students can see how much they have learned from class activities and discussions.

Continued.

EVALUATION—Cont'd.

This is How Well Our Group Did

Name _____   **Date** _____

1. The people in my group are_____
_____

2. We finished _____
_____
_____

3. This is how we cooperated.

	YES	SOMETIMES	NEVER
a. We planned well.			
b. We shared our ideas.			
c. We listened to each other.			
d. We encouraged each other.			
e. We shared materials.			

4. This is how I cooperated.

	YES	SOMETIMES	NEVER
a. I helped plan carefully.			
b. I shared my ideas.			
c. I listened to others.			
d. I encouraged others.			
e. I shared materials.			

5. I learned _____
_____
_____
_____

Figure 3.22 Student self-evaluation checklist.

3. The teacher might ask students to write short paragraphs that tell which part of the unit they enjoyed the most and what was learned from that activity.

4. Students are asked to choose their best pieces of writing done during the unit. The piece might be a poem, an imaginary story, or a factual report. Because students are using the writing process, they are assessing their own work regularly. The selection they choose as the best should be a final copy, ready for publication or presentation at the program planned for parents.

The teacher's evaluation of the unit is a continuous, ongoing process. The teacher should evaluate each day's activities and make written comments after each lesson or activity has been completed. This daily assessment of student learning should be used to guide and modify daily planning. As the teacher reflects, questions to be asked are:

1. What about the lesson worked well?
2. Were all of the children successful?
3. Did I meet my objectives?
4. What could I have done differently?
5. How could I have prepared better?
6. What new ideas did I get from the children that I could use the next time I teach the unit?

When the unit is finished, the teacher should reflect on the total experience.

1. Was the length of time appropriate?
2. Were we able to meet all of our goals and objectives?
3. What would I change?
4. How have my students grown?
5. How have I grown?

The teacher evaluates students through a variety of techniques. Daily work, individual projects, and group projects, as well as reading and writing assignments, should be used to get a total picture of each student's growth during the unit. For this unit the evaluation is based upon two main techniques: teacher observations and student portfolios.

Observations

The teacher should record daily comments about each individual student's learning. These observations might become data on a checklist or a simple note placed in a student portfolio. There are many opportunities for assessing

Continued.

EVALUATION—Cont'd.

Teacher Checklist for Independent Reading

Name _____   Date _____

Literacy Activities	Almost Always	Sometimes	Never
1. Chooses books at his or her reading level			
2. Reads and understands books chosen			
3. Completes book diary entries to the best of his or her ability			
4. Contributes thoughtful comments to group when discussing core books			
5. Shows enjoyment and willingness to read			
6. Listens attentively and responds to peer comments in discussions			
7. Completes literature-related activities on time and to the best of his or her ability			
8. Displays a growing vocabulary about unit topic			
9. Can use reading strategies emphasized during unit (*predicting*)			
10. Takes good care of books			

Figure 3.23 Teacher checklist for independent reading.

children's learning in this unit. The teacher should listen to students read, listen to them as they share pieces of writing with the class, watch them as they discuss core books within their small groups, listen to them as they retell stories they have read, and watch them as they solve problems or plan projects.

Portfolios

The portfolio should contain pieces that tell the most about each student. It could also contain unusual or special pieces selected by the student or the teacher. It should include:

1. A vocabulary list of new words from class sets. Each student's ocean dictionary would provide the basis for this list. The student is asked to demonstrate understanding of each work in context during a teacher-student conference.

2. The student's book diary containing the name of each book read independently, the date it was finished, and a few sentences describing something special about the book. The student's evaluation should be based on a goal set by the student and the teacher for the minimum number of books to be read. The teacher should collect diaries each week and write a response to student entries. A checklist could be used to gain further information about each student's independent reading.

3. Daily journal entries. These provide examples of student growth in writing skills but also give the teacher new and personal insights about each student.

4. Samples of student writing including poems, reports, and stories. Thank-you letters or invitations sent to parents could also be selected. The teacher and the student should collaboratively select items to be included in the portfolio.

5. Ocean learning log. The teacher assesses each student's summary of science, math, or social studies concepts taught during the unit. Logs also contain checklists or summaries of experiments related to this unit.

6. Projects and/or records of projects. Photographs, written comments by the student, and information gathered from student-teacher conferences should be included.

7. A unit test might be considered; however, the culminating activity of asking students to share what they learned about oceans, combined with the learning log, may provide the teacher with sufficient information to assess knowledge gained.

Continued.

EVALUATION—Cont'd.

Writing Checklist for Teacher Evaluation of Student

Name _____   Date _____

Literacy Activities	Almost Always	Sometimes	Never
1. Willingly attempts different kinds of writing emphasized in unit (poetry, reports, etc.)			
2. Can independently choose a topic			
3. Brainstorms ideas for writing			
4. Attempts to proofread and correct mechanics to the best of his or her ability			
5. Attempts to revise content to the best of his or her ability			
6. Shows improved spelling			
7. Reveals growing vocabulary, including key words from unit			
8. Is willing to ask for advice from peers			
9. Shows improvement in use of writing mechanics			
10. Shares writing with others			
11. Chooses to write outside school			

Figure 3.24 Writing checklist.

CHILDREN'S BOOKS CITED

Butterworth, O. (1987). *The enormous egg.* New York: Dell.

dePaola, T. (1990). *Little Grunt and the big egg.* New York: Holiday.

Scieska, J. (1989). *The true story of the three little pigs.* New York: Scholastic.

Van Allsburg, C. (1988). *Two bad ants.* Boston: Houghton Mifflin.

Carle, E. (1988). *A house for hermit crab.* Jefferson City, MO: Scholastic.

McGovern, A. (1979). *Little whale.* New York: Four Winds.

Allamand, P. (1979). *The animals who changed their colors.* New York: Lothrup, Lee and Shepard.

Peet, B. (1965). *Kermit the hermit.* Boston: Houghton Mifflin.

National Geographic books for young explorers, Exploring the seashore. (1984). Washington, DC: National Geographic Society.

National Geographic books for young explorers, Animals that live in the sea. (1978). Washington, DC: National Geographic Society.

National Geographic books for young explorers, The Wonderful world of seals and whales. (1984). Washington, DC: National Geographic Society.

Bush, J., & Paul, C. (1991). *The fish who could wish.* Brooklyn, NY: Kane/Miller.

Himmelman, J. (1990). *Ibis: The true whale story.* New York: Scholastic.

McDonald, M. (1990). *Is this a house for a hermit crab?* New York: Orchard.

Roop, P., & Roop, C. (1985). *Keep the lights burning, Abbie.* Minneapolis, MN: Carolrhoda.

Tresselt, A. (1965). *Hide and seek fog.* New York: Mulberry.

Kipling, R. (1952). *The crab that played with the sea (Just so stories).* New York: Doubleday.

Lionni, L. (1968). *Swimmy.* New York: Pantheon.

Cole, J. (1992). *The magic school bus on the ocean floor.* New York: Scholastic.

Simon, S. (1990). *Oceans.* New York: Morrow Junior Books.

MacDonald, G., & Weisgard, L. (1946). *The little island.* New York: Scholastic.

Rowland, D. (1990). *Explorer books: Sharks.* New York: Trumpet Club.

Andersen, H. C. (1974). *The little mermaid.* New York: Doubleday.

Waters, J. (1979). *A jellyfish is not a fish.* New York: Crowell.

Ehlert, L. (1990). *Fish eyes.* New York: Trumpet Club.

Milton, J. (1989). *Whales: The gentle giant.* New York: Random House.

Behrens, J. (1989). *Dolphins.* Chicago: Children's Press.

Pope, J. (1990). *Seahorses: Nature club series*. Mahwah, NJ: Troll Associates.

Lionni, L. (1970). *Fish is fish*. New York: Dragonfly.

Most, B. (1980). *My very own octopus*. New York: Harcourt Brace Jovanovich.

Nakawatari, H. (1990). *The sea and I*. New York: Farrar, Straus and Giroux.

Pallotta, J. (1986). *The ocean alphabet book*. Watertown, MA: Charlesbridge.

Tokuda, W., & Hall, R. (1986). *Humphrey, the lost whale (A true story)*. Union City, CA: Heian International.

Hulme, J. N. (1991). *Sea squares*. New York: Hyperion Books for Children.

Marshak, S. (1991). *I am the ocean*. New York: Little, Brown and Company.

Clements, A. (1988). *Big Al*. New York: Scholastic.

Donnelly, J. (1987). *The Titanic: Lost . . . and found*. New York: Random House.

Gibbons, G. (1988). *Sunken treasure*. New York: Harper Collins.

Bowden, J. C. (1979). *Why the tides ebb and flow*. Boston: Houghton Mifflin.

Doubilet, A., & Doubilet, D. (1991). *Under the sea from A to Z*. New York: Crown.

Sheldon, D. (1990). *The whale's song*. New York: Dial.

Grover, W. (1990). *Dolphin adventure*. New York: Greenwillow.

Conley, A. (1991). *Window on the deep: The adventures of the underwater explorer Sylvia Earle*. New York: Franklin Watts.

Simon, J. (1991). *My friend whale*. New York: Bantam.

Cooney, B. (1988). *Island boy*. New York: Trumpet Club.

Jacobs, F. (1992). *Sam the sea cow*. New York: Walker & Company.

Jennings, T. (1989). *The young scientist investigates sea and seashore*. Oxford: Oxford University Press.

Williams, V. B. (1988). *Stringbean's trip to the shining sea*. New York: Scholastic.

Kovacs, D. (1987). *A day underwater*. New York: Scholastic.

Holling, C. (1948). *Seabird*. Boston: Houghton Mifflin.

Turkle, B. (1969). *Thy friend Obadiah*. New York: Trumpet Club.

Pallotta, J. (1986). *The underwater alphabet*. Watertown, MA: Charlesbridge.

Pallotta, J., & Bolster, R. (1990). *Going lobstering*. Watertown, MA: Charlesbridge.

Poetry

Daniel, M. (Ed.) (1986). *A child's treasury of seaside verse.* New York: Dial.

Hopkins, L. B. (1986). *The sea is calling me.* New York: Harcourt Brace Jovanovich.

Shannon, G. (1989). *Sea gifts.* Boston: David R. Godine.

Ciardi, J. (1989). *The hopeful trout and other limericks.* Boston: Houghton Mifflin.

REFERENCES CITED

Graves, D., & Hansen, J. (1983). The author's chair. *Language Arts, 60,* 176–182.

Ogle, D. (1986). K-W-L: A teaching model that develops active reading of expository text. *Reading Teacher, 39,* 564–570.

4

PRACTICAL CONSIDERATIONS

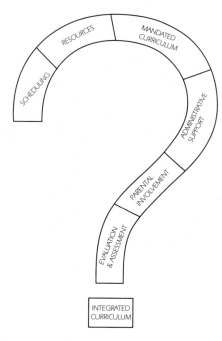

Figure 4.1 Graphic overview for Part Four.

INTRODUCTION

In *Designing Thematic Units: Process and Product*, we have attempted to demonstrate a flexible, workable process for creating thematic units to assist teachers and their students in the development of a literature-based, child-centered focus for instruction. Although the teachers who have used this model find it appropriate for their needs, they have raised a number of concerns and questions regarding the use of thematic units in general in elementary classrooms. As we sorted through these questions and concerns, we found that they fell into the following areas: scheduling, resources, mandated curriculum, administrative support, parental involvement, and evaluation and assessment. This chapter examines each of these areas of concern and offers suggestions to assist teachers in addressing these concerns within their schools and classrooms.

SCHEDULING

The school day is full of many activities. Certainly, the main objective for both teachers and students is to investigate and learn about a variety of subjects. However, other activities also vie for teachers' and students' attention. In the elementary school, students often leave the classroom for physical education, music, art, library, and special classes such as resource room or remedial reading. Additionally, there are countless other interruptions to instructional time. Class pictures must be taken, eyes and ears must be examined, and visiting speakers must be heard. Teachers find that they have little time available for planning or learning about new methodologies and ideas. Inservice and preservice teachers with whom we have worked to develop thematic units have asked many questions directly related to the time required for the development and implementation of thematic units. Samples of their questions are given next; answers and suggestions to meet the concerns expressed in the questions follow.

1. How can I cover all of the material that I must and still schedule literature-based units?
2. How do I work around special programs and classes, such as computer and music?
3. How can I schedule student conferences and feedback sessions for twenty-five students and meet everyone's needs in one day?
4. When do I schedule planning time?

Question 1. How can I cover all of the material that I must and still schedule literature-based units? Teachers often think that using thematic units adds to the amount of information or the number of lessons they must include each day. In reality, all of the information and content that the teacher would normally cover during a lesson or unit of study are incorporated into the thematic unit. For example, if the teacher planned to teach about transportation in social studies, addition and subtraction calculations in math, and the environment in science, she might include all of these topics in a thematic unit in which one group of students chose to calculate the amount of natural and manufactured resources required by a conveyance of their choice. Literature resources could include *Tin Lizzies* (Spier, 1975), *Cars* (Royston, 1991), *Going on an Airplane* (Rogers, 1989), *Train Song* (Siebert, 1990), and *Bus Stop Boys* (Kingsland, 1991). Thus, by combining several content areas within one unit and by using literature as the bridge, or connector, the teacher makes better use of the available instructional time.

Question 2. How do I work around special programs and classes, such as computer and music? In the classrooms in which we have talked or visited, we have noticed that children leave the classroom at various times to receive instruction from special teachers such as music teachers, physical education teachers, learning disabilities or reading specialists, or computer specialists. Although some schools are moving toward an inclusion model to meet the needs of all children, other teachers are still faced with a fragmented curriculum. These constant disruptions often leave teachers with their class intact for only a few hours each day. Teachers are naturally concerned about adding more disruptions to an already busy day. In our work with teachers we have found that thematic units actually lessen the stress related to students' comings and goings. Once the unit has been introduced and students have decided their particular course of action or group of activities, the need for large blocks of time with the entire class is minimized. Rather than a hindrance, thematic units generally allow the teacher increased flexibility. Developing some classroom management strategies to help keep track of which students are gone from the classroom at particular times allows the teacher to focus more attention on providing instructional support.

Question 3. How can I schedule student conferences and feedback sessions for twenty-five students and meet everyone's needs in one day? It is important, whether using thematic units or other methods of instruction, for a teacher to consider and meet the needs of all children in the class. For busy teachers, this is often the most difficult and frustrating aspect of teaching. The teachers who have expressed their concerns with us worry that thematic units require each student to be involved in an individual activity. However, in reality, there are many opportunities within the framework of thematic units that encourage children to collaborate and consult with one another. Thematic units are a perfect instructional tool if the teacher is planning cooperative learning groups. The teacher who becomes less of an instructional director and more of a facilitator finds more opportunities during the day to interact with students to offer feedback and suggestions and to assess student and unit progress.

We have found that the following techniques assist teachers in managing their classrooms when children are engaged in a variety of activities.

1. Whenever children are engaged in a group activity, provide the group with a tape recorder and ask that they record their discussion or activity. The teacher can later listen to the tape and determine if the group needs personal guidance or materials and books. This practice also offers the teacher opportunities to assess student progress and gives students the opportunity to complete self-assessments.

Figure 4.2 A bulletin board management system.

2. Develop a monitoring system in which children indicate on a bulletin board display, a poster, or the blackboard where they will be for the period or what activity they will be pursuing. The students should assume the responsibility for informing the teacher of the plan of action. Not only does this help the teacher with management issues but also it allows the students to develop ownership of and responsibility for their own learning.

3. Encourage students to seek help and information from their peers. Often their classmates can provide insight into which resources (books, encyclopedias, magazines, and other materials) are the most helpful, or they can assist with tasks such as proofreading and editing.

4. Have a place on the blackboard or wall where children can sign up for a teacher conference. Rather than the teacher checking with each child every day, the children indicate when they need assistance or are ready to share.

Question 4. When do I schedule planning time? Planning with thematic units is much different than the type of planning usually associated with classroom instruction. Traditional planning is generally done in isolation. By contrast, thematic planning is most effectively completed in concert with others. Depending on the teacher's particular situation, planning might be accomplished by working in a team effort with other teachers or by supporting students as they select a topic and develop activities and resources related to it. Collaborative teacher planning might occur before and after school or during a scheduled planning period. Planning with students should be an integral part of daily activities in a literature-based classroom. In the models we present in this text, a teacher or group of teachers is most often involved in the initial planning, and students are given opportunities to make choices or to suggest activities and projects they would like to pursue. Granting students a more active role in planning with increased responsibilities for selection of topic and resources is the ultimate goal; however, in situations in which the teacher is concerned or required to meet specific curriculum goals and outlines, the teacher may make some initial decisions related to topic. Also, because teachers are more familiar with what resources are available, it is often more helpful if they do the initial scouting for materials. This, of course, does not preclude students from making decisions or suggesting and supplying materials and resources. Teachers will find the implementation of thematic units easier and more successful if they consider themselves part of a team of learners that includes other teachers and students. Figures 4.3 and 4.4 are examples of daily schedules for primary and intermediate grades.

Daily Schedule, Primary Grades

8:15–8:30	Organize (lunch money, attendance, etc.)
8:30–8:50	Teacher reads
8:50–9:15	Class meeting
	Check homework
	Daily objectives
	Daily news
9:15–9:45	Teacher-directed, language arts–related lesson
	Uses teacher-read book or theme-related literature
	Addresses theme-related objectives
9:45–10:30	Reading-writing workshop
	Independent reading
	Independent writing (at various stages of writing process)
	Core book reading (small groups)
	Partner reading
	Teacher-student conferences
	Peer conferences
10:30–10:40	Break
10:40–11:00	Content lesson
	Math, science, and/or social studies
	Minilesson with practice
	May be theme related
11:00–11:45	Lunch
11:45–12:00	Sharing time
	Author's chair
	Book talks
	Reader's theater
12:00–12:15	Journal entries
12:15–12:30	Minilesson, theme related
	Addresses specific unit objectives
12:30–1:30	Reading-writing workshop
	Independent reading
	Guided reading
	Independent writing (at various stages of writing process)
	Sharing of reading or writing
1:30–2:00	Out-of-class activities (art, music, physical education)
2:00–2:30	Theme projects
2:30–2:45	Wrap up
	Homework
	Sharing of afternoon accomplishments
	Self-evaluation
2:45–3:00	Teacher reads
3:00	Students dismissed

Figure 4.3 Daily schedule for primary grades.

Daily Schedule Intermediate Grades

8:00–8:15	Organize (details, attendance, lunch, etc.)
8:15–8:30	Teacher reads
8:30–8:45	Class meeting
	What are you working on?
	What are your goals for the day?
	Homework check
8:45–9:00	Minilesson (reading, writing, or literature selection)
9:00–10:15	Reading-writing workshop (may be theme related)
	Read core books
	Teacher-student conferences
	Read self-selected books
	Peer conferences
	Responding activities
	Literature circles
10:15–11:00	Out-of-class activities (physical education, music, art)
11:00–11:45	Content area instruction related to theme
	Math, science, and/or social studies
	Minilesson
	Related activities (individual or small group)
11:45–12:15	Lunch
12:15–12:30	Journal work
12:30–12:45	Group sharing of morning work
12:45–1:15	Whole class instruction, theme related
	Content lesson, reading-writing lesson
	Addresses specific unit objectives
1:15–2:15	Theme-related activities
	Group projects
	Individual projects or activities
	Content-related projects
	Teacher-student conferences
2:15–2:30	Wrap up
	Self-evaluation
	Homework
2:30–3:00	Sharing
	Book talks, author's chair, reader's theater, project presentations
3:00–3:15	Teacher reads
3:15	Students dismissed

Figure 4.4 Daily schedule for intermediate grades.

RESOURCES

An important consideration when planning thematic units is locating and displaying resources. As discussed in Part One, having a literacy-rich environment is important even if the teacher does not use thematic units. However, teachers often see the use of thematic units as demanding more resources than those already located in the classroom. Because one of the primary considerations in the development of thematic units is the use of a variety of resource materials, this section is devoted to suggestions for locating, obtaining, and displaying resources. Specific suggestions for books and materials related to selected themes and general teacher resources can be found in the Appendices. When contacting various agencies, organizations, or businesses, the teacher should also consider asking about guest speakers, field trips, and classroom exhibits.

When teachers are trying to locate materials for student use, they look for good-quality materials that fit into a limited budget. (Part Two discusses criteria for selection.) Sources of free or inexpensive materials are especially appreciated. The following list provides sources most often used by the authors and by the teachers and students with whom we have worked. Readers are encouraged to expand and refine this list.

1. *School library:* This is a much-overlooked source for classroom materials. The school library media specialist can assist the teacher or the students in locating books, videos, and tapes related to selected themes. Being included in the planning team alerts the library media specialist to topics that the children will be researching and enables the staff to make appropriate reference materials readily available.

2. *Colleagues.* Other teachers in the building may allow the teacher to borrow copies of books to create class sets or books that fit within a selected theme. As teachers begin to plan thematic units together, they can share resources and help to develop a common professional and classroom library.

3. *Public library.* Teachers are usually allowed to check out more books or to have them for extended times. Teachers should also encourage students to utilize the public library for their research.

4. *Family and friends.* Many times families and friends have books they no longer want that are stored in attics and garages. Making your needs known to them could net books, magazines, maps, and brochures.

5. *School book clubs for children.* These clubs offer discounts and free books to teachers, depending on the number of books that their students order. Big books, maps, reference books, and other classroom equipment can be bought or earned.

6. *Used bookstores.* Almost every town has a secondhand bookstore. Prices are less than what a person would pay in a regular bookstore, and often the store is willing to trade. This is an excellent place to take books that have been discarded by friends and family but are not appropriate for classroom use.

7. *Garage sales.* Locating materials and resources at garage sales can be a real adventure! It is easy to find excellent paperback children's books for as little as a quarter. Also, do not overlook the possibility of finding back issues of magazines, globes, play props, manipulatives, and bookshelves.

8. *Business partners.* Some businesses will donate a specific resource to the classroom, such as a one-year subscription to a children's magazine or a class set of books. Check with parents about the possibility of establishing such partnerships with the companies for which they work.

9. *Newspaper offices.* A classroom subscription to the local newspaper is sometimes offered by the newspaper office. Even if the newspaper is furnished only one day a week, the resource can be a valuable addition. You might also be able to obtain blank end rolls of newsprint, which can be used for murals, storyboards, and other artwork.

10. *Government agencies.* Brochures and informational newsletters can be obtained by writing to government offices. State departments of tourism offer beautiful pamphlets of the historical and popular sites within the state. Check also with such agencies as departments of transportation for maps, archives for historical records, and census bureaus for statistics.

11. *Embassies and consulates.* If your unit involves research about other countries, the embassy or consulates for that country can provide brochures and information.

12. *Travel agencies.* They are good sources for posters, maps, brochures, and information.

13. *Nonprofit organizations.* Organizations such as the Heart Association, the Lung Association, and the Easter Seals Foundation are happy to supply teachers and students with information related to prevention and treatment of specific diseases and disorders.

14. *Corporations.* Many large companies are happy to provide information related to their product as part of their public relations program. For example, candy companies might provide an informational brochure on how chocolate is made, an automobile manufacturer might send a history of the automobile in America, or a clothing manufacturer

might send a poster of how cotton is made into cloth. A word of warning: these materials should be carefully screened to eliminate any that simply promote the sale of the product.

Once books and other materials have been selected and obtained as possible resources for a particular theme, the teacher should display them in a manner that makes them inviting and accessible to the students. Within the classroom there should be a quiet reading area established where children can browse through books and other printed materials undisturbed. Research indicates that children are more attracted to materials if the covers can be seen; therefore, shelving in the reading area should allow some of the books to be displayed in this manner (Morrow, 1993). Videos and cassettes can be best utilized in a designated listening or viewing area. There should also be areas that allow children to share and discuss the resources they have located with other children in the class. (Refer to Part One for a discussion of the importance of a supportive literacy-rich environment.)

MANDATED CURRICULUM

Most states have developed a statewide curriculum that each school district must follow. These curricula usually address the same concepts, skills, and attitudes evaluated by standardized tests. Failure to meet these mandated curricula could cause districts to lose financial and instructional support from the state. Therefore, it should be easy to understand why many teachers are concerned that changing the way they teach will have some impact on their ability to meet state or district curriculum mandates. Teacher concerns revolve around three issues: (1) requirements related to *what* will be taught; (2) requirements related to *how* information will be taught, that is, basal readers, state-approved textbooks, and the like; and (3) requirements related to *when* and *how much* will be taught in any specific grade.

Some districts have stricter guidelines for compliance than others. We have been in districts that have developed checklists of guidelines and criteria of successful completion. Some districts even list textbook and workbook pages related to the topic! In these districts, administrators routinely check teachers' written plans and observe actual classroom interactions to document that the guidelines and criteria are being met. Other districts simply list topics that are to be covered in each grade. By providing basal textbooks, these districts hope to guarantee that the guidelines are being met. Whatever the situation in which teachers find themselves regarding an established curriculum, we believe that thematic units can be a useful tool for meeting those requirements.

As outlined in Part Two, after the teacher or the teacher and students select a model and a focus and have brainstormed ideas related to them, the curriculum guidelines are consulted to see in which areas there might be a match. The teachers with which we have worked have generally been surprised that there have been so many ways to incorporate their mandated curriculum guidelines into the topics and activities they and their students really want to pursue. Thematic units provide teachers and students with the means to engage in meaningful learning and still be in compliance with district and state wishes. In many cases, the teachers discover that they are able to cover more material than is mandated and in greater depth than they had anticipated.

ADMINISTRATIVE SUPPORT

Acquiring and maintaining administrators' support for classroom instructional techniques and activities are important for the success of any program. It is imperative for the teacher who wishes to implement thematic units to gain that support.

Teachers with whom we have worked have encountered two types of problems when trying to gain administrative support for their work. First is the difficulty of establishing an instructional dialogue with the principal if such a dialogue has not been ongoing. Teachers should begin talking with administrators about their views of learning long before they ask support for making any changes or adaptations in the instructional pattern. They should strive to share with the principal examples of children's work and to involve the principal in the community of learners in the classroom. Some teachers have found it helpful to ask principals to read aloud to their classes, to visit displays of work, to attend performances of readers' theater or plays, and to share their own areas of expertise. An administrator who knows and respects teachers' work is more likely to support them in new endeavors because trust relationships have already been developed.

A second and more crucial problem that a teacher might encounter with an administrator is a conflict between the teacher's philosophy of learning and the administrator's philosophy of learning. Perhaps the principal believes that children learn best when they are sitting in their desks and focused on the individual work in front of them. The principal might believe that noise and movement by the students cause a disruption in learning. In addition, the principal would like to see the teacher giving out the information and testing to ensure that students have mastered the information. Such a principal might not understand the philosophy that supports student construction of meaning through self-guided activities, let alone peer assessment, self-assessment, or portfolio assessment. Teachers working with such an administrator might find it difficult to implement thematic units into the curriculum without the principal's support.

The question, then, is how to move in the direction of understanding and

Figure 4.5 Teachers and administrators are team players.

respecting each other's philosophies. Information and education are the keys. Teachers might initiate conversations in which they discuss the benefits of using thematic units and in which they reassure the principal that curriculum goals can still be met. Regularly sharing articles about thematic units and integrated instruction from professional journals and books with the principal can provide teachers with research support for their arguments. Teachers may want to enlist the principal in the planning of a small unit, perhaps a literature supplement unit, and provide the principal with feedback as the children progress. Nothing convinces like success; student progress eventually convinces wary administrators of the value of thematic, integrated instruction.

PARENTAL INVOLVEMENT

Equally as important as acquiring the support and understanding of administrative personnel is gaining the support of the parents of the students in your classroom. Parents often need and want information related to what their child is accomplishing in the classroom. As with any new project or assignment, parents need to be informed of the purpose and projected outcomes of the thematic units you implement in the classroom. Because many parents are more accustomed to traditional instruction that includes worksheets, homework assignments, and unit tests, they need information related to the types of activities in which their child is engaged and the means of assessment and evaluation that will be utilized. The teacher should schedule parent workshops that provide parents with information as well as opportunities to engage in actual instructional activities similar to the ones their children are experiencing.

Teachers may find it most helpful to enlist parental participation within the classroom. Parents can help teachers in the areas of assisting students, locating resources, providing expert information, supplying materials, and maintaining records. Parents who are actively involved in the learning community are more supportive of the teacher's use of thematic units and can often gain support from other parents in ways that are unavailable to the teacher.

A second way to involve parents is to provide them with frequent information regarding the projects involving students. The students in the classroom may want to help the teacher produce and distribute a class newsletter (Figure 4-6). A newsletter assures parents that productive work is occurring within the classroom and gives them many opportunities to offer their assistance. Progress reports and notes to specific parents keep them from becoming concerned that their child is not involved in meaningful learning activities and alerts them to areas of concern.

Parent Pages: A Newsletter from Mrs. Allen's Class

Dear Parents,

These nine weeks our class will be studying oceans. We will be reading many books, such as *The Magic School Bus on the Ocean Floor*, *Why the Tides Ebb and Flow*, *Humphrey the Lost Whale*, and *The Titanic: Lost . . . and Found*, among others.

We will be creating an ocean seascape in one corner of our room. If you have fishnets, shells, or other ocean articles that you could contribute, please send or bring them to the school. We can also use some help cutting paper and hanging our "kelp" forest.

The class has divided into six groups, and each group will be doing a research project. We are excited about looking for books and magazines to help us in our reports. If you have books about the ocean you can lend us, we promise to take very good care of them.

We have a special surprise planned for the last week of our unit. We'll keep you posted so you can make plans to join us during that week.

We are excited about our work and invite you to share in the excitement. If you can volunteer time, supplies, books, or expertise, please call Mrs. Allen at 555-1234.

Figure 4.6 Sample page from weekly newsletter.

EVALUATION AND ASSESSMENT

Teachers have many concerns related to the assessment and evaluation of both the students' work and the unit itself. Some of the questions that we have been asked are:

1. How do I evaluate students' work without daily assignments and test scores?
2. How do I find the time to adequately assess progress?
3. How do I evaluate the success of the thematic unit related to goals set by the teacher and the students and to the objectives and mandates of the curriculum?
4. How does this type of evaluation and assessment fit required tests, such as achievement tests?
5. How do I know if the self-assessment and peer evaluations are valid?

All of these questions are important to consider in light of the requirements of states and districts to meet specific performance criteria. A teacher would be foolish not to consider these requirements as important. However, just as important as providing documentation related to state requirements is the need to provide the teacher and students feedback about the success of their unit and information about individual growth and knowledge.

We have found in our work that the most successful method for documenting student growth and knowledge over time is to assist the students in compiling a portfolio with representative work samples. Portfolios allow the student to provide evidence of the reading and writing process as well the product of the process, to include both formal and informal measures, and to view the student's work within the context of the learning environment (Anthony, Johnson, Mickelson, & Preece, 1991). The nature of this handbook does not allow us to discuss portfolio assessment in great depth. Readers can refer to References Consulted at the end of Part Four for excellent books and articles on this topic. To summarize the topic, however, documents that might be appropriate for inclusion in a student portfolio include:

1. Pictures and descriptions of projects
2. Project reports
3. Lists of resources consulted
4. Checklists
5. Learning log and/or response journal entries
6. Self-assessments
7. Group and peer assessments
8. Audiotapes of oral reading or group discussions
9. Videotapes of individual or group presentations

Examples of several of these are given in the units in Part Three of this text. The student should have the primary responsibility for selecting materials, but the teacher will also want to include observations in the form of either anecdotes or checklists. The teacher and student may also want to ask parents to comment on the portfolio contents periodically.

The teacher will also want to keep notes and observation checklists to assess the effectiveness of the activities for promoting learning. Examples are provided in Figure 4.8 and in Part Three of this text. The teacher will also want to make note of which resources were most helpful and which provided little help. A teacher who is just beginning to implement thematic units might ask a colleague or administrator to observe class activities and provide feedback about the teacher's role in the activities. As an additional

Student Planning Sheet

Name: _____   Theme: _____
Date Started: _____   Date Finished: _____

MY OWN GOALS

What do I want to do?	How well did I do?
1.	1.
2.	2.
3.	3.
4.	4.

PROJECTS

Individual	Started	Checkup	Finished	How well did I do?
1.				
2.				
Group				
1.				
2.				

ACTIVITIES

Activities	Partner(s)	Started	Checkup	Finished	How well did I do?

Figure 4.7 Student planning sheet.

source of information, the teacher should also ask the students to evaluate the unit. Periodically, students can comment in their learning logs about what they are learning or what has been helpful to their learning (Figures 4-9 and 4-10). A summary checklist or individual paragraphs in which each student states what was good about the study and what was not good can be useful to the teacher in future planning.

SUMMARY

In Part Four we have addressed concerns and questions that teachers might have about the implementation of thematic units as a method of instruction. Major areas of concern were scheduling thematic units, location and display of resources, mandated curriculum requirements, administrative support, parental support, and assessment and evaluation issues. We presented suggestions and examples to facilitate the use of thematic units to assist teachers as they deal with these practical considerations on a day-to-day basis.

Unit Evaluation

Unit _____ Dates _____

	Yes	No
1. Students were actively engaged throughout the unit.		
2. Student attitudes remained positive.		
3. Students had opportunities to read, write, listen, & speak.		
4. Work was challenging.		
5. Content objectives were met.		
6. There were sufficient resources.		
7. Time frame was appropriate.		

Activity   **Comments**

Figure 4.8 Sample of unit evaluation.

Student's Daily Log

Unit _____ Name _____

Week One:

Activity _____

Comments _____

_____

_____

Activity _____

Comments _____

_____

_____

Activity _____

Comments _____

_____

_____

Activity _____

Comments _____

_____

_____

Activity _____

Comments _____

_____

_____

Figure 4.9 Student's daily learning log.

Student Activity Record

Name _____ Theme _____

Teacher assigned activities or projects	Date Started	Date Completed
1. Create a character map		
2. Write a report		
3. Build a model		
4.		

Student selected activities and projects	Date Started	Date Completed
1. Write a play		
2. Create a wire sculpture		
3. Sing a song		
4.		
5.		

Student Comments: _____

_____

_____

Teacher Comments: _____

_____

_____

Figure 4.10 Student activity record.

REFERENCES CITED

Anthony, R. J., Johnson, T. D., Mickelson, N. I., & Preece, A. (1991). *Evaluating literacy: A perspective for change.* Portsmouth, NH: Heinemann.

Morrow, L. M. (1993). *Literacy development in the early years.* Boston: Allyn and Bacon.

REFERENCES CONSULTED

Flood, J., & Lapp, D. (1989). Reporting reading progress: A comparison portfolio for parents. The Reading Teacher, 43, 508–514.

Glazer, S. M., & Brown, C. S. (1993). *Portfolios and beyond: Collaborative assessment in reading and writing.* Norwood, MA: Christopher Gordon.

Machado, J. M. (1990). *Early childhood experiences in language arts.* New York: Delmar.

McGee, L. M., & Richgels, D. J. (1990). *Literacy's beginnings: Supporting young readers and writers.* Boston: Allyn and Bacon.

Mills, H., & Clyde, J. A., Eds. (1990). *Portraits of whole language classrooms.* Portsmouth, NH: Heinemann.

Moore, D. W., Moore, S. A., Cunningham, P. M., & Cunningham, J. W. (1986). *Developing readers and writers in the content areas.* New York: Longman.

Pace, G. (1991). When teachers use literature for literacy instruction: Ways that constrain, ways that free. *Language Arts, 68,* 12–25.

CHILDREN'S BOOKS CITED

Kingsland, R. (1991). *Bus stop boys.* New York: Viking.

Rogers, F. (1989). *Going on an airplane.* New York: Putnam.

Royston, A. (1991). *Cars.* New York: Aladdin Books.

Siebert, D. (1990). *Train song.* New York: Crowell.

Spier, P. (1975). *Tin lizzies.* New York: Doubleday.

5

POSITIVE RESULTS

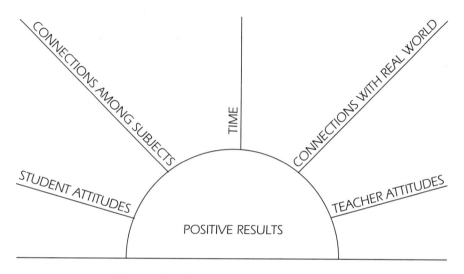

Figure 5.1 Graphic overview for Part Five.

INTRODUCTION

Literature-based thematic units can provide a framework for moving away from fragmented or isolated instructional units or time periods to integrated contexts for learning. "Perhaps the most compelling reason to teach with themes [however] is that, done well, they promote a view of both teaching and learning as meaningful enterprise" (Lipson, Valencia, Wixson, & Peters, 1993, p. 253). In that context, we believe there are five important benefits for teachers who decide to use literature-based themes.

141

TIME

We are experiencing a knowledge explosion, and children are expected to learn more and more facts. Teachers are expected to fit more topics into the curriculum and at the same time make way for "extra" activities for their students, be they stringed instrument lessons, cultural studies, drug awareness education, or square dancing. "I just don't have enough time to teach" or "My students never have enough time to complete anything because they are always going out of the classroom for something special" are complaints frequently heard from many classroom teachers today.

Using thematic literature-based units gives teachers a way to handle the ever-increasing demands on their teaching and decision-making skills. "By combining several separate curricular areas and reducing redundancy in the process, teachers and students should not only have more time but better quality time: time that is less fragmented and available in larger blocks" (Lipson et al., 1993, p. 254). For example, a unit whose theme centers on prejudice could include specific concepts from the social studies, like American Civil War history, Hitler's treatment of the Jews, or modern U. S. history of the civil rights movement, as well as specific language arts strategies and skills. A large block of time set aside for student investigations, reading, writing, and creating projects or teacher-directed minilessons could easily pull together social studies concepts and literature in a meaningful setting. A setting such as this allows skills to be taught in the context of authentic student needs. There would be no separate history (social studies), writing, or reading period, but a time for students to engage in real reflective thinking and learning. In a classroom where children are focusing on an environmental theme, they could select from books like *The Great Kapok Tree* (Cherry, 1990), *On the Far Side of the Mountain* (George, 1990), or *Song of the Seahorse* (Base, 1992) for independent reading time; these books could then become the motivation for journal writing or story telling or even the stimulus for doing independent research into a related real-life environmental problem. These books could also be the basis for a teacher-directed science lesson directed toward humans' responsibility for their environment.

When a teacher gains control over the time factor, students might actually have time to make choices and really enjoy their own reading and writing. A teacher would not have to choose between giving children time to read authentic literature or teach that social studies lesson. The teacher would not have to give up self-selected or sustained silent reading and writing because they would be a natural part of the overall skeletal plan for the unit.

Explicit instruction (teaching time) would be evident, but it would be well selected and employed to maximize time for students and teachers to learn together. Minilessons aimed at skills or strategies needed for successful learning of specific content could be included in the unit planning, or

Figure 5.2 Creating a classroom rainforest is one way to encourage children to make connections.

they might occur as a result of needs evidenced by students during their investigations.

Using themes does not necessarily mean that more time is available. If literature-based themed units are added to the curriculum without changing other aspects of the program, teachers will have more included in an already crowded day and be convinced that thematic units are only enrichment or just plain too much work. However, if they truly "reduce the number of subjects by embedding one in another" (Lipson et al., 1993, p. 255), then quality time becomes available for authentic, meaningful teaching and learning that is long term and personal in nature.

CONNECTIONS BETWEEN CONTENT AREAS

Literature-based units can provide students and teachers with a coherence that might not be possible if subjects are taught separately. Such units can provide a framework (focus) for what is to be taught and learned. We know that "students who cannot see meaningful connections across content or skill areas . . . are unlikely to be able to use their knowledge and skills to solve problems or make decisions" (Lipson et al., 1993, p. 253). Using literature as a vehicle for teaching content often helps students gain a deeper understanding. As Cooper (1993) suggests, "The ability to both construct meaning and to gain content knowledge is enhanced by thinking about and engaging in cross-curricular learning" (p. 501), the kind that we believe comes with well-planned, thematic, literature-based units. Reading and writing in response to literature-based themes encourage students to gain understanding that has greater depth and breadth (Pappas, Kiefer, & Levstik, 1990). Guzzetti, Kowalinski & McGowan (1992) suggest that students can acquire more concepts and greater understanding of those concepts through literature-based instruction. Furthermore, "literature can frequently provide students with causal relationships [not always visible in content text] and give readers an opportunity to engage in self-questioning and critical thinking" (p. 115).

Such instruction frequently helps students understand why they are doing what they are doing. They see how work in reading or writing might help them in science or social studies. It is also likely to result in a greater transfer of knowledge and discovery of connections. Second-grader Kara said during a science lesson on the ocean, "Oh, I already know that. I read in *The Magic School Bus on the Ocean Floor* [Cole, 1992] that the ocean floor isn't flat at all. It has mountains and valleys that are even bigger than ones we can see on the earth." Fifth-grader Josh commented after reading *Shades of Gray* (1989) by Carolyn Reeder, "I think I see now why it was so hard for the United States to pull together after the Civil War. Some families had sons or uncles fighting for the North and brothers fighting for the South. If they had to live with that, it must have been very hard for the whole country to get back together." Spiro, Vispoel, Schmitz & Boerger (1987) even suggest that when a topic has been "traversed and crisscrossed" (p. 195) from many perspectives, students acquire an integrated knowledge base that allows them to recall information more quickly and to be more flexible problem solvers. When speaking of using an integrated approach to curriculum planning, Perkins (1989) summarizes, "Students' understanding within subject matters should become deeper, their understanding of the relationships among subject matters should become sharper, and their thinking should become more insightful and systematic, in school and out" (p. 76). All of this points to long-term results: enhanced background knowledge, greater depth of understanding, and genuine connections across subject lines.

Children know that the real world is not divided into separate disciplines; they see the world as a whole. Using thematic units allows students to make connections among subjects as they see them in the real world.

CONNECTIONS WITH THE REAL WORLD

Using thematic units presumes an active role for children in the learning process. They should have a variety of options from which to choose that reflect their interests and abilities. Although at times the teacher may select the focus, children should be involved in locating resources that are of interest to them and in selecting response projects that meet their interests and needs. They might choose activities suggested by the teacher, activities suggested during a class brainstorming session, or activities of their own, such as creating plays, writing and publishing stories, planning a newscast, creating a choral production, solving a problem, or simply sharing new insights with a friend.

The active involvement of students encourages them to approach a theme from the vantage point of their own world. McGowen and Guzetti (1991) suggest that tradebooks used in literature-based social studies thematic units help students "relate their ordinary-life experiences and prior knowledge to the content concepts" and facilitates the "understanding of new information" (p. 17). Norton (1991) indicates that "books of non-fiction encourage children to look at the world in new ways, to discover laws of nature and society, and to identify people different from themselves" (p. 608). In other words, children have the opportunity to view problems from different perspectives and to see human relationships in a real-life context. Children who read *From Anna* (Little, 1972) might easily identify with Anna's feelings about being different; second graders who read *Wilfrid Gordon McDonald Partridge* (Fox, 1985) might have an older friend or grandparent in a nursing home and find that the book evokes very personal emotions about the wonderful relationship illustrated in the book. Reading *Come*

Figure 5.3 Current informational texts provide children with connections to the real world.

a Stranger (Voigt, 1986) or *Child of the Owl* (Yep, 1977) often gives intermediate-grade children an opportunity to reflect on prejudice in a very personal manner; these books make the study of immigration or diversity more meaningful.

Because students see connections among subject areas in thematic units of study, they can also understand that their learning has application to real life, to real topics—that learning is not just isolated bits of fact in a vacuum. When students do make these connections with their own lives and their own world, they are able to transfer their knowledge and strategies to new learning situations.

TEACHER ATTITUDES

Teachers, too, are positively affected by using themed literature-based units. First of all, planning literature-based units is a task that requires complex decisions; this "gives teachers an enormous sense of empowerment and satisfaction" (Tompkins & McGee, 1993, p. 305). Greater teacher satisfaction results from knowing that the themes selected and activities suggested provide students an opportunity for learning that is personally meaningful to them.

Teaching with themed literature-based units also fosters collaboration among teachers and builds a sense of community among teachers (George & Alexander, 1993, p. 284). Teachers who work together develop a "new understanding and respect for [all] content areas" and a "collaborative spirit" (Willis, 1992, p. 3). The result is positive attitudes toward teaching and

Figure 5.4 Teacher-student collaboration brings satisfaction.

toward their peers. Jacobs (1989) refers to this spirit as "collegiality." She also suggests that when more sharing is apparent, a "sense of pride and accomplishment" is also present (p. 50).

Teachers who have chosen to use literature-based thematic units have also expressed a renewed interest in teaching. George and Alexander (1993) have shared comments from middle-school teachers whose involvement in curriculum integration has motivated them to see their own teaching from a more positive perspective (p. 288). A young teacher with whom the authors worked noted,

> Using children's literature in my classroom has really opened up a whole new world to me. I am rereading books I read as a child and enjoying them again. I am reading books I never had an opportunity to read. It's like I'm able to recapture a part of my own childhood. Sharing my own enthusiasm about literature with my students has been wonderful. I am always looking for ways to integrate literature into subject areas; it seems that the possibilities are endless. (Manhart, L., personal communication, 1993, April).

The effects of this kind of genuine enthusiasm for teaching will certainly be evident in the teaching and learning environment.

Although these affective benefits are not easily documented, "they too are real" (Vars, 1984, p. 50). Evidence shows that motivation is a key factor in the learning environment; we know as well that the teacher's role in motivation is crucial. A sense of pride, a feeling of community, and a newfound joy in teaching all contribute toward a positive teaching and learning environment.

STUDENT ATTITUDES

Perhaps the most often named benefit of teaching with literature-based thematic units is that it can promote positive student attitudes. We have already demonstrated that literature-based instruction encourages students to discover connections within and among content areas; this way of learning parallels the way they see the world—whole. When instruction is more authentic and more "attuned to the way children and adults learn" (Hughes, 1991, p. 11.), positive attitudes result. Students have an opportunity to see their learning "in a context of real world significance" and are often inspired "to want to know more" (Reutzel & Cooter, 1992, p. 429).

Students should have a "voice" in the development and implementation of thematic units (Oldfather, 1993, p. 672). This voice gives them opportunities to pursue special interests or use individual skills in carrying out activities related to the chosen theme. They have opportunities to work and plan with their classmates and build a sense of cooperation and community within their own classroom. Students feel important; they, too, are decision

Figure 5.5 Teachers enjoy reading children's literature too.

Figure 5.6 Reading good literature is fun.

Figure 5.7 *A community of readers.*

makers. In effect, they are empowered and have control over their own learning. Oldfather (1993) says that children become "personally invested and connected to their literacy activities" (p. 673). Such a personal investment gives students that inner motivation that all teachers strive to encourage and a positive attitude toward learning. A sixth-grade boy who was asked to read *Hatchet* (Paulsen, 1987) as part of a thematic unit on courage became so excited upon finding a book he really enjoyed that he asked his teacher to tell him the names of other books by Gary Paulsen and began to read them one after another. He shared his enthusiasm about these books with his friends, and soon they also became Paulsen fans.

SUMMARY

Although we have addressed each benefit separately, each is really deeply embedded in the others. When students are highly motivated and the experiences they are having are personally meaningful and relevant to real life, they learn more readily (Holdaway, 1982), transfer learning from one context to another (Lipson et al., 1993), and are more likely to acquire the strategies that make for long-term, in-depth learning (Pappas et al., 1990). In classrooms where teachers collaborate with their peers and with their students, all are engaging in teaching and learning in a meaningful context (Lipson et al., 1993). We believe that literature-based thematic units can be the vehicle for such a rewarding enterprise.

REFERENCES CITED

Calfee, R. C. (1987). *The role of text structure in acquiring knowledge.* Final report to the U.S. Department of Education (Federal Program No. 122B) Palo Alto, CA: Stanford University.

Cooper, J. D. (1993). *Literacy: Helping children construct meaning.* Boston: Houghton Mifflin.

George, P. S., & Alexander, W. M. (1993). *The exemplary middle school* (2nd ed.). New York: Harcourt Brace Jovanovich.

Graves, D. H. (1991). *Build a literature classroom.* Portsmouth, NH: Heinemann.

Guzzetti, B. J., Kowalinski, B. J., & McGowan, T. (1992). Using a literature-based approach to teaching social studies. *Journal of Reading, 36,* 114–121.

Holdaway, D. (1982). Shared book experience: Teaching reading using favorite books. *Theory into practice, 21,* 293–300.

Hughes, M. (1991). *Curriculum integration in the primary grades: A framework for excellence.* Alexandria, VA: Association for Supervision and Curriculum Development.

Jacobs, H. H. (1989). Descriptions of two existing interdisciplinary programs. In H. H. Jacobs (Ed.), *Interdisciplinary curriculum: Design and implementation* (pp. 39-52). Alexandria, VA: Association for Supervision and Curriculum Development.

Lipson, M. Y., Valencia, S. W., Wixson, K. K., & Peters, C. W. (1993). Integration and thematic teaching: Integration to improve teaching and learning. *Language Arts, 70,* 252–263.

L. Manhart (personal communication, April 1993).

McGowan, T., & Guzetti, B. (1991). Promoting social studies understanding through literature-based instruction. *The Social Studies, 82,* 16–21.

Norton, D. E. (1991). *Through the eyes of a child: An introduction to children's literature* (3rd ed.). New York: Macmillan.

Oldfather, P. (1993). What students say about motivating experiences in whole language classrooms. *The Reading Teacher, 46,* 672–681.

Pappas, C. C., Kiefer, B. Z., & Levstik, L. S. (1990). *An integrated language arts perspective in the elementary school.* New York: Longman.

Perkins, D. N. (1989). Selecting fertile themes for integrated learning. In H. H. Jacobs (Ed.), *Interdisciplinary curriculum: Design and implementation* (pp. 67-76). Alexandria, VA: Association for Supervision and Curriculum Development.

Reutzel, D. R., & Cooter, R. B. (1992). *Teaching children to read: From basals to books.* New York: Merrill.

Spiro, R. J., Vispoel, W. P., Schmitz, A. S., & Boerger, A. E. (1987). Knowledge acquisition for application: Cognitive flexibility and transfer in complex content domains. In B.K. Britton and S. M. Glynn (Eds.), *Executive control and process in reading* (pp. 177-197). Hillsdale, NJ: Erlbaum.

Tompkins, G. E., & McGee, L. M. (1993). *Teaching reading with literature: Case studies to action plans.* New York: Macmillan.

Vars, G. F. (1984). *A bibliography of research on the effectiveness of block-time, core, and interdisciplinary team teaching programs.* Kent, OH: National Association for Core Curriculum.

Willis, S. (1992). Interdisciplinary learning: Movement to link the disciplines gains momentum. In *Curriculum update.* Alexandria, VA: Association for Supervision and Curriculum Development.

REFERENCES CONSULTED

Brozo, W. G., & Tomlinson, C. M. (1986). Literature: The key to lively content courses. *The Reading Teacher, 40,* 288–293.

Buckley, M. C. (1986). When teachers decide to integrate the language arts curriculum. *Language Arts, 63,* 369–377.

Coodman, K. S., Hood, W. J., & Goodman, Y. M. (1991). *Organizing for whole language.* Portsmouth, NH: Heinemann.

Hansen, J. (1987). *When writers read.* Portsmouth, NH: Heinemann.

Hiebert, E. H., & Colt, J. (1989). Patterns of literature-based reading instruction. *The Reading Teacher, 41,* 14–20.

James, M., & Zarillo, M. (1989). Teaching history with children's literature: A concept-based interdisciplinary approach. *The Social Studies, 80,* 153–158.

Moss, B. (1991). Children's nonfiction tradebooks: A complement to content area texts. *The Reading Teacher, 45,* 26–32.

Newman, J. M. (1985). *Whole language theory and use.* Portsmouth, NH: Heinemann.

Pace, G. (1991). When teachers use literature for literacy instruction: Ways that constrain, ways that free. *Language Arts, 68,* 12–25.

Routman, R. (1988). *Transitions: From literature to literacy.* Portsmouth, NH: Heinemann.

Routman, R. (1991). *Invitations: Changing as teachers and learners K–12.* Portsmouth, NH: Heinemann.

Stewig, J. L., & Sebesta, S. L. (Eds.). (1989). *Using literature in the elementary classroom.* Urbana, IL: National Council for Teachers of English.

Vars, G. E. (1991). Integrated curriculum in historical perspective. *Educational Leadership, 49,* 14–15.

CHILDREN'S BOOKS CITED

Base, G. (1992). *Song of the seahorse.* New York: Harry N. Abrams.

Cherry, L. (1990). *The great kapok tree.* New York: Trumpet.

Cole, J. (1992). *The magic school bus on the ocean floor.* New York: Scholastic.

Fox, M. (1985). *Wilfrid Gordon McDonald Partridge.* Brooklyn, NY: Kane/Miller.

George, J. C. (1990). *On the far side of the mountain.* New York: Trumpet.

Little, J. (1972). *From Anna.* New York: Harper & Row.

Paulsen, G. (1987). *Hatchet.* New York: Trumpet.

Reeder, C. (1989). *Shades of gray.* New York: Avon.

Voigt, C. (1986). *Come a stranger.* New York: Ballantine.

Yep, L. (1977). *Child of the owl.* New York: Harper & Row.

6

PUTTING IT ALL TOGETHER

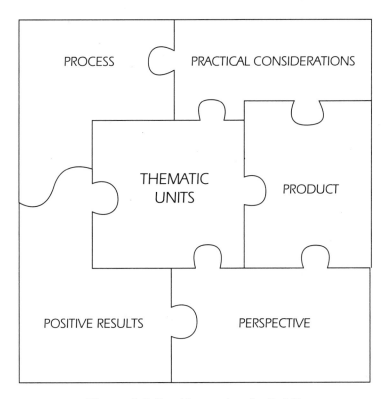

Figure 6.1 Graphic overview for Part Six.

Teachers and children in many classrooms are engaging in an exploration of their worlds set in the context of authentic literacy experiences. They are sharing the spotlight as they plan together, read together, and respond to their reading in ways that are very personal and exciting.

Students who are participating in thematic units are constructing meaning and gaining knowledge about literature and content areas; they are

Figure 6.2 Teachers and children enjoy the world of books.

learning to build relationships among subject areas in the curriculum. They are becoming successful as readers, writers, and thinkers as they respond to authentic literature. They are excited about school and about learning.

Teachers who are attempting to create thematic units are rediscovering the world of children's literature; they are personally engaged in the reading and writing process, modeling reading strategies for their students, collaborating with their students and with fellow teachers, and supporting their students' learning. They are finding new excitement in curriculum integration as they use literature-based thematic units.

Although some teachers are successfully planning and using thematic units, many questions about literature-based instruction remain unanswered. We developed this handbook to help both preservice and inservice teachers as they sort through the literature, define their own beliefs about teaching and learning, and attempt to build thematic units that demonstrate a consistency between learning theory and classroom practice. We believe our handbook is unique because it does just that.

In Part One we presented the foundation on which this book was written. We shared with you our beliefs about teaching and learning and outlined the principles of literacy learning that support the use of literature-based instruction. Next we examined the roles of both the classroom teacher in supporting literacy development and the student who engages in literacy activities. We described a literacy-rich environment that nurtures children's growth and demonstrated the natural role literature should have in that environment. We then defined *thematic units* in a manner consistent with our belief system. Using this definition set in a literacy-rich environment, we began to share with you a unique process for creating thematic units.

In Part Two of this handbook, we presented a step-by-step approach to the process of integrating literature and then attempted to lead teachers through that process in building thematic units. We provided three different models teachers might use in unit planning. Teachers might choose to use model 1, the literature supplement model, in which literature is used as a supplement to content area instruction; model 2, the literature-centered model, which begins with a specific piece of literature; or model 3, the literature-infused model, which represents a balance between the use of children's literature and the use of concepts selected from all content areas. We then followed teacher Dorothy as she used the process in building a unit based on model 2, often sharing with the reader Dorothy's thoughts as she made decisions about her unit.

Part Three contains three possible unit plans that were created by the process described in Part Two. Although these three units seem complete, it is not our intent to provide a packaged product for teachers to use. It is our

Figure 6.3 An authentic literacy experience.

belief that children should be involved in making many decisions in planning and implementing literature-based units. It is also our belief that each unit that results from the use of this process should be tailored to meet the needs of a specific teacher and a specific group of students. We included a sample unit for each model to demonstrate the flexibility of using our process of building literature-based units. We expect that any teacher who chooses to use one of the unit plans would see it as just a beginning that would be modified to meet the needs of the students.

From our work with preservice and inservice teachers, we realize that there are some practical issues teachers may face as they attempt to plan for literature-based instruction. In Part Four we have attempted to address some of the concerns teachers shared with us. Choosing to use children's literature as a vehicle for developing thematic units of study is a complex issue. It requires teachers to make conscious decisions about issues such as scheduling constraints, the availability of resources, mandated curriculum requirements, the need for vigorous administrative support, the importance of parental involvement, and finally evaluation and assessment strategies and methods that are consistent with the way children learn.

Part Five provides a positive conclusion to our handbook. Although teachers do face complex decisions when implementing this process, there are real benefits to using thematic literature-based instruction in the classroom. We would encourage teachers to make discriminating decisions and to respond to their students' needs and interests. Literature-based instruction built around meaningful themes can provide the vehicle to do just that and at the same time promote the view that teaching and learning are part of a meaningful experience. Thematic units, as we have described and modeled them:

- Allow children to make connections between and among content areas
- Give children an opportunity to apply reading strategies in authentic contexts
- Make use of and expand background knowledge
- Support collaborative and cooperative learning
- Integrate all of the language arts
- Allow children to construct language and knowledge in an active, social environment
- Bring excitement and enthusiasm to teachers and students

Themes and Related Literature for Primary Children

THEME 1: DINOSAURS
Teacher Resources

Books

Rountree, B. S., Taylor, N. Y., & Shuptrine, M. B. (1989). *Where are the dinosaurs?* Tuscaloosa, AL: The Learning Line.

Videos

Dinosaur Bob & His Adventures with the Family Lazardo. Reading Rainbow.

Children's Resources

Children's Fiction Books

Adler, D. A. (1988). *The dinosaur princess and other prehistoric riddles.* New York: Holiday House.

Barnes, B. (1990). *Bones, bones, dinosaur bones.* New York: Thomas Y. Crowell.

Burton, V. L. (1967). *Mike Mulligan and his steam shovel.* New York: Scholastic.

Carrick, C. (1983). *Patrick's dinosaurs.* New York: Clarion Books.

Donnelly, L. (1990). *Dinosaur garden.* New York: Scholastic.

Hennessey, B. G. (1988). *The dinosaurs who lived in my backyard.* New York: Viking Kestrel.

161

Joyce, W. (1988). *Dinosaur Bob and his adventures with the family Lazardo.* New York: Harper & Row.

Kellogg, S. (1987). *Prehistoric Pinkerton.* New York: Dial Books.

Morgan, M. (1991). *Dinostory.* New York: Dutton Books.

Most, B. (1987). *Dinosaur cousins?* San Diego: Harcourt Brace Jovanovich.

Most, B. (1989). *The littlest dinosaurs.* San Diego: Harcourt Brace Jovanovich.

Most, B. (1990). *Four & twenty dinosaurs.* New York: Harper & Row.

Taylor, S. (1990). *Dinosaur James.* New York: Morrow Junior Books.

Children's Nonfiction Books

Aliki. (1985). *Dinosaurs are different.* New York: T. Y. Crowell.

Aliki. (1988). *Digging up dinosaurs.* New York: T. Y. Crowell.

Aliki. (1990). *Fossils tell of long ago.* New York: T. Y. Crowell.

Branley, F. M. (1989). *What happened to the dinosaurs?* New York: T. Y. Crowell.

Cole, J. (1974). *Dinosaur story.* New York: Morrow.

Hornblow, L., & Hornblow, A. (1974). *Prehistoric monsters did the strangest things.* New York: Random House.

Most, B. (1984). *Whatever happened to dinosaurs?* San Diego: Harcourt Brace Jovanovich.

Penner, L. R. (1991). *Dinosaur babies.* New York: Random House.

Schlein, M. (1991). *Discovering dinosaur babies.* New York: Four Winds Press.

Stout, W. (1981). *The dinosaurs: A fantastic new view of a lost era.* New York: Bantam Books.

Children's Magazines

Zoobooks—Dinosaurs. Vol. 9, No. 12, September 1992.

THEME 2: INTERGENERATIONAL RELATIONSHIPS

Teacher Resources

Videos

The Patchwork Quilt. Reading Rainbow.

Children's Resources

Children's Fiction Books

Bahr, M. (1992). *The memory box.* Morton Grove, IL: Albert Whitman & Co.

Brandenberg, F. (1975). *A secret for grandmother's birthday.* New York: Greenwillow Books.

Burningham, J. (1984). *Grandpa.* New York: Crown Publishers.

Caseley, J. (1990). *Grandpa's garden lunch.* New York: Greenwillow Books.

Cech, J. (1991). *My grandmother's journey.* New York: Bradbury Press.

Crews, D. (1991). *Bigmama's.* New York: Trumpet.

DePaola, T. (1973). *Nana upstairs & nana downstairs.* New York: Trumpet.

Flora, J. (1978). Grandpa's ghost stories. Hartford, CT: Atheneum.

Fox, M. (1985). *Wilfrid Gordon Mcdonald Partridge.* Brooklyn, NY: Kane/Miller Book Publishers.

Gould, D. (1987). *Grandpa's slide show.* New York: Lothrop, Lee & Shepard.

Greenfield, E. (1988). *Grandpa's face.* New York: Trumpet.

Houston, G. (1992). *My great aunt Arizona.* New York: Harper Collins.

Howard, E. F. (1991). *Aunt Flossie's hats (and crab cakes later).* New York: Clarion Books.

Johnston, T. (1988). *Yonder.* New York: Dial Books for Young Readers.

Lasky, K. (1979). *My island grandma.* New York: Frederick Warne.

Martin, B. Jr., & Archambault, J. (1987). *Knots on a counting rope.* New York: Trumpet.

Munsch, R. (1990). *Love you forever.* Willowdale, Ontario: Firefly Books.

Newman, S. P. (1979). *Tell me Grandma, tell me Grandma.* Boston: Houghton Mifflin.

Rylant, C. (1985). *The relatives came.* New York: Bradbury Press.

Wahl, J. (1976). *Great-grandmother cat tales.* New York: Dell.

Wahl, J. (1981). *Grandpa Gus's birthday cake.* Englewood Cliffs, NJ: Prentice-Hall.

THEME 3: WEATHER

Teacher Resources

Videos

Bringing the Rain to Kapiti Plain. Reading Rainbow.

Snowy Day. Reading Rainbow.

Children's Resources

Children's Fiction Books

Barrett, J. (1978). *Cloudy with a chance of meatballs.* New York: Atheneum.

Chesworth, M. (1992). *Rainy day dream.* New York: Farrar, Straus & Giroux.

Keats, E. J. (1964). *The snowy day.* New York: Viking Press.

Martin, B. Jr. (1967). *Weather.* New York: Holt, Rinehart & Winston.

Children's Nonfiction Books

Fowler, A. (1991). *What's the weather today?* Chicago: Children's Press.

Gibbons, G. (1987). *Weather forecasting.* New York: Four Winds.

Gibbons, G. (1990). *Weather words and what they mean.* New York: Holiday House.

Gikofsky, I. (1992). *Don't blame the weatherman.* New York: Avon.

THEME 4: FRIENDS

Teacher Resources

Videos

Best Friends. Reading Rainbow.

My Little Island. Reading Rainbow.

Children's Resources

Children's Fiction Books

Aliki. (1982). *We are best friends.* New York: Greenwillow Books.

Kellogg, S. (1986). *Best Friends.* New York: Trumpet.

Lobel, A. (1979). *Days with frog and toad.* New York: Harper & Row.

Silverstein, S. (1964). *The giving tree.* New York: Harper & Row.

Children's Nonfiction Books

Rogers, F. (1987). *Making friends.* New York: Putnam.

THEME 5: FOLKTALES
Teacher Resources
Videos
Abiyoyo. Reading Rainbow.

Bringing the Rain to Kapiti Plain. Reading Rainbow.

The Gift of the Sacred Dog. Reading Rainbow.

The Legend of the Indian Paintbrush. Reading Rainbow.

The Tortoise and the Hare. Reading Rainbow.

Children's Resources
Children's Fiction Books
Aardema, V. (1975). *Why mosquitoes buzz in people's ears.* New York: Dial Press.

Aardema, V. (1989). *Rabbit makes a monkey of lion.* New York: Dial Books for Young Readers.

Aliki. (1963). *The story of Johnny Appleseed.* New York: Trumpet.

Bowden, J. C. (1979). *Why the tides ebb and flow.* Boston: Houghton Mifflin.

Harris, J. C. (1986). *Jump! The adventures of Brer Rabbit.* San Diego: Harcourt Brace Jovanovich.

Kimmel, E. A. (1988). *Anansi and the moss-covered rock.* New York: Holiday.

McDermott, G. (1992). *Zomo the rabbit: A trickster tale from West Africa.* San Diego: Harcourt Brace Jovanovich.

Searcy, M. Z. (1978). *Alligator gets a bump on his nose.* Tuscaloosa, AL: Portals Press.

Searcy, M. Z. (1978). *Tiny bat and the ballgame.* Tuscaloosa, AL: Portals Press.

Children's Nonfiction Books
Durrell, A. (1989). *The Diane Goode book of American folk tales and songs.* New York: E. P. Dutton.

THEME 6: INSECTS
Teacher Resources
Videos
Bugs. Reading Rainbow.

The Life Cycle of the Honeybee. Reading Rainbow.

Children's Resources

Children's Fiction Books

Carle, E. (1987). *The very hungry caterpillar*. New York: Philomel.

Fleischman, P. (1985). *Joyful noise: Poems for two voices*. New York: Trumpet.

Heller, R. (1983). *The reason for a flower*. New York: Grossett & Dunlap.

Hepworth, C. (1992). *Antics*. New York: Trumpet.

Ryder, J. (1977). *Fireflies*. New York: Harper & Row.

Van Allsburg, C. (1988). *Two bad ants*. Boston: Houghton Mifflin.

Children's Nonfiction Books

Dorros, A. (1987). *Ant cities*. New York: T. Y. Crowell.

Hawes, J. (1967). *Ladybug, ladybug, fly away home*. New York: T. Y. Crowell.

Hogan, P. Z. (1979). *The Honeybee*. Milwaukee: Raintree Children's Books.

Lang, S. S. (1992). *Invisible bugs and other creepy creatures that live with you*. New York: Sterling.

Parker, N. W., & Wright, J. R. (1987). *Bugs*. New York: Greenwillow Books.

THEME 7: TRANSPORTATION

Teacher Resources

Videos

The Adventures of Taxi Dog. Reading Rainbow.

The Bicycle Man. Reading Rainbow.

Children's Resources

Children's Fiction Books

Crews, D. (1982). *Harbor*. New York: Greenwillow Books.

Crews, D. (1985). *Bicycle race*. New York: Greenwillow Books.

Gibbons, G. (1983). *Boat book*. New York: Holiday House.

Howard, E. F. (1988). *The train to Lulu's*. New York: Bradbury Press.

Kingsland, R. (1991). *Bus stop boys*. New York: Viking.

McPhail, D. M. (1977). *The train*. Boston: Little, Brown.

Siebert, D. (1990). *Train song*. New York: T. Y. Crowell.

Spier, P. (1975). *Tin lizzie*. New York: Doubleday.

Children's Nonfiction Books

Baer, E. (1990). *This is the way we go to school*. New York: Scholastic.

Baker, E. H. (1969). *I want to be a taxi driver*. Chicago: Children's Press.

Barner, B. (1990). *The elevator/escalator book*. New York: Doubleday.

Bauer, J. (1990). *What's it like to be an airline pilot?* Mahweh, NJ: Troll Associates.

Cole, J. (1983). *Cars and how they go*. New York: Crowell.

Crews, D. (1986). *Flying*. New York: Greenwillow Books.

Folsom, M. (1965). *Keep your eyes open*. New York: Grossett & Dunlap.

Gibbons, G. (1987). *Trains*. New York: Holiday House.

Magee, D. (1985). *Trucks you can count on*. New York: Dodd, Mead.

Morris, A. (1990). *On the go*. New York: Lothrop, Lee & Shepard Books.

Rogers, F. (1989). *Going on an airplane*. New York: Putnam.

Royston, A. (1991). *Cars*. New York: Aladdin Books.

THEME 8: SEASONS

Children's Resources

Children's Fiction Books

Barklem, J. (1980). *Autumn story*. New York: Philomel Books.

Barklem, J. (1980). *Spring story*. New York: Philomel Books.

Barklem, J. (1980). *Winter story*. New York: Philomel Books.

DePaola, T. (1977). *Four stories for four seasons*. Englewood Cliffs, NJ: Prentice Hall.

Goennel, H. (1986). *Seasons*. Boston: Little, Brown.

Hertz, O. (1984). *Tobias goes ice fishing*. Minneapolis: Carolrhoda.

Johnston, T. (1988). *Yonder*. New York: Dial Books for Young Readers.

Maestro, B. (1985). *Through the year with Harriet*. New York: Crown Publishers.

Parnall, P. (1986). *Winter barn*. New York: Macmillan.

Rockwell, A. (1985). *First comes spring*. New York: Crowell.

Rylant, C. (1987). *Henry and Mudge in puddle trouble*. New York: Bradbury Press.

Rylant, C. (1987). *Henry and Mudge in the green time*. New York: Bradbury Press.

Rylant, C. (1987). *Henry and Mudge under the yellow moon.* New York: Bradbury Press.

Zolotow, C. (1975). *The summer night.* New York: Harper.

Children's Nonfiction Books

Beer, K. C. (1977). *What happens in the spring.* Washington, DC: National Geographic Society.

Howell, R. R. (1972). *Everything changes.* New York: Atheneum.

Marshak, S. (1983). *The month-brothers.* New York: William Morrow.

Selsam, M. E. (1982). *Where do they go?* New York: Four Winds Press.

THEME 9: FAMOUS PEOPLE
Children's Resources
Children's Nonfiction Books

Adler, D. A. (1989). *A picture book of Abraham Lincoln.* New York: Trumpet.

Adler, D. A. (1989). *A picture book of Martin Luther King, Jr.* New York: Holiday House.

Adler, D. A. (1990). *A picture book of Helen Keller.* New York: Trumpet.

Adler, D. A. (1991). *A picture book of John F. Kennedy.* New York: Holiday House.

Aliki. (1988). *The many lives of Benjamin Franklin.* New York: Simon & Schuster.

Davidson, M. (1964). *The story of Thomas Alva Edison, inventor: The wizard of Menlo Park.* New York: Scholastic.

Epstein, S., & Epstein, B. (1980). *She never looked back: Margaret Mead in Samoa.* New York: Coward.

THEME 10: FAIRY TALES
Teacher Resources
Videos

Beauty and the Beast. Walt Disney.

The Little Mermaid. Walt Disney.

Rumplestiltskin. Reading Rainbow.

Children's Resources

Children's Fiction Books

Anderson, H. C. (1989). *The little mermaid.* New York: Harcourt Brace Jovanovich.

Appleby, E. (1984). *The three billy-goats gruff.* New York: Scholastic.

Brett, J. (1989). *Beauty and the beast.* New York: Trumpet.

Cauley, L. B. (1979). *The ugly duckling.* New York: Harcourt Brace Jovanovich.

Hayes, S. (1985). *Hansel and Gretel and other stories.* New York: Derrydale Books.

Hayes, S. (1985). *Puss in boots and other stories.* New York: Derrydale Books.

Hyman, T. S. (1983). *Little red riding hood.* New York: Holiday House.

Kellogg, S. (1985). *Chicken little.* New York: Trumpet.

Scieszka, J. (1991). *The frog prince continued.* New York: Trumpet.

Tarcov, E. H. (1973). *Rumpelstiltskin.* New York: Scholastic.

Themes and Related Literature for Intermediate Children

The suggested themes in this appendix were determined by analyzing current textbooks for grades three through six for topics, by reviewing several states' curriculum guidelines for those grades, and by our work with students and student teachers. The books were chosen by reviewing such notable lists as Children's Choices (International Reading Association), Teachers' Choices (IRA), Newbery winners, and various reference books for library media specialists. These books and themes are intended only as starting points for teachers and students for building appropriate thematic units for the intermediate grades. Teachers may want to expand a unit idea with additional books or combine these ideas with new ones to create new thematic units.

THEME 1: JOURNEYS

Children's Resources

Children's Fiction Books

Baum, L. F. (1987). *The wonderful world of Oz*. New York: Morrow.

Burnford, S. (1990). *The incredible journey*. New York: Bantam.

Cole, J. (1989). *The magic school bus inside the earth*. New York: Scholastic.

Corcoran, B. (1970). *The long journey*. New York: Atheneum.

Dahl, R. (1961). *James and the giant peach*. New York: Puffin Books.

Hunt, I. (1987). *Up a road slowly.* New York: Berkeley Publishing.

Joffo, J. (1974). *A bag of marbles.* Boston: Houghton Mifflin.

Juster, N. (1988). *The phantom tollbooth.* New York: Knopf.

Kroll, S. (1981). *Giant journey.* New York: Holiday House.

Lenski, L. (1966). *Judy's journey.* New York: Dell.

Lewis, C. S. (1988). *The lion, the witch, and the wardrobe.* New York: Macmillan.

Lewis, C. S. (1961). *Voyage of the dawn treader.* New York: Macmillan.

MacLachlan, P. (1991). *Journey.* New York: Doubleday.

O'Dell, S. (1973). *Sing down the moon.* New York: Dell.

Pinkwater, D. (1989). *Guys from space.* New York: Macmillan.

Steele, M. Q. (1979). *Journey outside.* New York: Puffin Books.

Uchida, Y. (1971). *Journey to topaz.* New York: Scribner's.

Williams, V. B. (1988). *Stringbean's trip to the shining sea.* New York: Greenwillow.

Children's Nonfiction Books

Baum, A., & Baum, J. (1987). *Opt: An illusionary tale.* New York: Viking.

Ride, S. (1989). *To space and back.* New York: Lothrop, Lee & Shepard.

THEME 2: IMMIGRATION

Children's Resources

Children's Fiction Books

Buss, F. (1991). *Journey of the sparrows.* New York: Dutton.

Coerr, E. (1993). *Chang's paper pony.* New York: Harper Collins.

Fritz, J. (1982). *Homesick: My own story.* New York: Dell.

Gilson, J. (1991). *Hello, my name is Scrambled Eggs.* New York: Minstrel.

Kherdian, D. (1979). *The road from home: The story of an Armenian girl.* New York: Scholastic.

Kingsley, E. P. (1986). *An American tail.* New York: Grossett & Dunlap.

Kroll, S. (1991). *Mary McLean and the St. Patrick's day parade.* New York: Scholastic.

Levinson, R. (1986). *Watch the stars come out.* New York: E. P. Dutton.

Lord, B. (1984). *The year of the boar and Jackie Robinson.* New York: Trumpet.

Milligan, B. (1987). *With the wind.* San Antonio: Corona Publishers.

Moskin, M. (1975). *Waiting for Mama.* New York: Coward.

Sonder, B. (1992). *Tenement writer: An immigrant's story.* Milwaukee: Raintree Steck Vaughn.

Yep, L. (1975). *Dragonwings.* New York: Harper & Row.

Children's Nonfiction Books

Finkelstein, N. H. (1989). *The other 1492: Jewish settlement in the new world.* New York: Scribner's.

Knight, J. (1982). *Sailing to America: Colonists at sea.* New York: Troll.

Kurelek, W., & Englehart, M. S. (1985). *They sought a new world: The story of European immigration to North America.* Plattsburgh, NY: Tundra Books.

Meltzer, M. (1976). *Taking root: Jewish immigrants in America.* New York: Farrar, Straus & Giroux.

Sherman, E. B. (1990). *Independence avenue.* Philadelphia: Jewish Publication Society.

THEME 3: WORLD WAR II

Teacher Resources

Audio

World War 2 (cassette tapes with actual radio broadcasts). National Archives Trust Fund Board.

Children's Resources

Children's Fiction Books

Arnothy, C. (1986). *I am fifteen and I don't want to die.* New York: Scholastic.

Bishop, C. H. (1978). *Twenty and ten.* New York: Puffin Books.

Choi, S. N. (1991). *Year of impossible goodbyes.* New York: Dell.

Coerr, E. (1977). *Sadako and the thousand paper cranes.* New York: Putnam.

Greene, B. (1973). *The summer of my German soldier.* New York: Bantam.

Uchida, Y. (1978). *Journey home.* New York: Atheneum.

Wolitzer, H. (1981). *Introducing Shirley Braverman.* New York: Dell.

Yolen, J. (1988). *The devil's arithmetic.* New York: Viking.

Children's Nonfiction Books

Adler, D. A. (1989). *We remember the holocaust.* New York: Henry Holt.

Black, B. (1992). *America at war! Battles that turned the tide.* New York: Scholastic.

Black, W. B., & Blashfield, J. F. (1991). *Pearl Harbor*. New York: Crestwood House.

Chaikin, M. (1992). *A nighttime in history: The holocaust*. Boston: Houghton Mifflin.

Dank, M. (1984). *Turning points of World War II: D-day*. New York: Franklin Watts.

Sullivan, G. (1991). *Day Pearl Harbor was bombed: A photo history of World War II*. New York: Scholastic.

THEME 4: COURAGE

Children's Resources

Children's Fiction Books

Arnold, E. (1975). *Brave Jimmy Stone*. New York: Scholastic.

Avi. (1984). *The fighting ground*. Philadelphia: J. B. Lippincott.

Brady, E. W. (1979). *Tolliver's secret*. New York: Avon.

Byars, B. (1970). *Summer of the swans*. New York: Viking.

Collier, J. L., & Collier, C. (1981). *Jump ship to freedom*. New York: Delacorte.

Dalgliesh, A. (1954). *Courage of Sarah Noble*. New York: Macmillan.

George, J. C. (1972). *Julie of the wolves*. New York: Trumpet.

Grollman, S. (1988). *Shira: A legacy of courage*. New York: Doubleday.

Keith, H. (1957). *Rifles for Watie*. New York: Harper Collins.

McDaniel, L. (1985). *Six months to live*. Worthington, OH: Willowisp.

Myers, W. D. (1988). *Fast Sam, Cool Clyde and stuff*. New York: Puffin.

O'Dell, S. (1982). *Sarah Bishop*. New York: Scholastic.

Patterson, K. (1991). *Lyddie*. New York: Trumpet.

Paulsen, G. (1987). *Hatchet*. New York: Trumpet.

Paulsen, G. (1991). *The river*. New York: Dell.

Speare, E. G. (1983). *Sign of the beaver*. New York: Dell.

Slote, A. (1975). *Hang tough, Paul Mather*. New York: Avon.

Children's Nonfiction Books

Krementz, J. (1989). *How it feels to fight for your life*. Boston: Little, Brown.

Lidz, R. (1980). *Many kinds of courage: An oral history of World War II*. New York: Putnam.

White, R., & Cunningham, A. M. (1991). *Ryan White: My own story*. New York: Dial.

THEME 5: PREJUDICE

Children's Resources

Children's Fiction Books

Blos, J. W. (1979). *A gathering of days: A New England girl's journal, 1830–1832.* New York: Scribner.

Lowry, L. (1989). *Number the stars.* New York: Dell.

Reeder, C. (1989). *Shades of gray.* New York: Avon.

Speare, E. G. (1958). *The witch of blackbird pond.* New York: Dell.

Taylor, M. D. (1990). *The road to Memphis.* New York: Dial.

Turner, A. (1987). *Nettie's trip south.* New York: Macmillan.

Uchida, Y. (1978). *Journey home.* New York: Atheneum.

Voigt, C. (1986). *Come a stranger.* New York: Ballantine.

Yep, L. (1977). *Child of the owl.* New York: Harper Collins.

Children's Nonfiction Books

Davis, D. S. (1982). *Behind barbed wire: The imprisonment of Japanese Americans during World War II.* New York: Dutton.

THEME 6: PEER RELATIONSHIPS

Children's Resources

Children's Fiction Books

Bulla, C. R. (1973). *Dexter.* New York: Crowell.

Byars, B. (1970). *Summer of the swans.* New York: Viking.

Byars, B. (1981). *The cybil war.* New York: Viking.

Cooney, C. B. (1988). *The girl who invented romance.* New York: Bantam.

Hahn, M. D. (1991). *Steppings on cracks.* New York: Avon.

Lowry, L. (1977). *A summer to die.* New York: Bantam.

Paterson, K. (1977). *Bridge to Terabithia.* New York: Trumpet.

Paulson, G. (1991). *The monument.* New York: Delacorte.

Reit, A. (1988). *I thought you were my best friend.* New York: Scholastic.

Snyder, Z. K. (1970). *The changeling.* New York: Atheneum.

Children's Nonfiction Books

Solomon, D. (1989). *Oh sister! Giggles, gasps & groans growing up together.* New York: Warner.

THEME 7: DIVERSITY

Children's Resources

Children's Fiction Books

Carter, F. (1976). *The education of Little Tree.* Albuquerque: University of New Mexico Press.

Charlip, R., & Beth, M. (1987). *Handtalk birthday: A number and story book in sign language.* New York: Four Winds.

Choi, S. N. (1991). *Year of impossible goodbyes.* New York: Dell.

Dooley, N. (1991). *Everybody cooks rice.* Minneapolis: Carolrhoda.

Edwards, M. (1992). *Alef-Bet: A Hebrew alphabet book.* New York: Lothrop, Lee & Shepard.

Flourney, V. (1985). *The patchwork quilt.* New York: Dial.

Keegan, M. (1991). *Pueblo boy: Growing up in two worlds.* New York: Dutton.

Lester, J. (1968). *To be a slave.* New York: Dell.

Little, J. (1972). *From Anna.* New York: Harper & Row.

Livingston, M. C. (1992). *Let freedom ring: A ballad of Martin Luther King, Jr.* New York: Holiday House.

Lord, B. B. (1984). *The year of the boar and Jackie Robinson.* New York: Harper & Row.

Mohr, N. (1977). *In Nueva York.* New York: Dell.

Mohr, N. (1983). *Nilda.* New York: Harper & Row.

Naylor, P. R. (1973). *To walk the sky path.* New York: Dell.

Peterson, J. W. (1977). *I have a sister, my sister is deaf.* New York: Harper Collins.

Polacco, P. (1992). *Chicken Sunday.* New York: Philomel.

Showers, P. (1991). *Your skin and mine.* New York: Harper Collins.

Smalls-Hector, I. (1991). *Irene and the big, fine nickel.* Boston: Little, Brown.

Sneve, V.D.H. (1972). *High Elk's treasure.* New York: Holiday.

Sneve, V.D.H. (1972). *Jimmy Yellow Hawk.* New York: Holiday.

Sneve, V.D.H. (1974). *When thunders spoke.* New York: Holiday.

Spier, P. (1990). *People.* New York: Doubleday.

Uchida, Y. (1981). *A jar of dreams.* New York: McElderry.

Uchida, Y. (1983). *The best bad thing.* New York: McElderry.

Uchida, Y. (1985). *The happiest ending.* New York: McElderry.

Voigt, C. (1986). *Come a stranger.* New York: Macmillan.

Whelan, G. (1991). *Hannah*. New York: Knopf.

Yep, L. (1977). *Child of the owl*. New York: Harper & Row.

Yep, L. (1979). *Sea glass*. New York: Harper & Row.

Children's Nonfiction Books

Farber, N. (1979). *How does it feel to be old?* New York: Dutton.

Giovanni, N. (1985). *Spin a soft black song*. New York: Farrar, Strauss & Giroux.

Meltzer, M. (1980). *The Chinese Americans*. New York: Crowell.

Meltzer, M. (1992). *The Hispanic Americans*. New York: Crowell.

Meltzer, M. (1982). *The Jewish Americans: A history in their own words*. New York: Crowell.

Meltzer, M. (1984). *The Black Americans: A history in their own words*. New York: Crowell.

Shaw, R., (Ed.). (1975). *Witch, witch! Stories and poems of sorcery, spells & hocus-pocus*. New York: Frederick Warne.

THEME 8: MYSTERY

Children's Resources

Children's Fiction Books

Adler, D. (1985). *Jeffrey's ghost and the 5th grade dragon*. New York: Henry Holt.

Adler, D. A. (1987). *My dog and the birthday mystery*. New York: Holiday.

Avi. (1993). *The true confessions of Charlotte Doyle*. Thorndike, ME: Thorndike.

Babbitt, N. (1970). *Knock knee rise*. New York: Trumpet.

Base, G. (1989). *The eleventh hour: A curious mystery*. New York: Abrams.

Berends, P. (1989). *The case of the elevator duck*. New York: Random House for Young Readers.

Bunting, E. (1986). *Someone is hiding on Alcatraz Island*. New York: Berkley.

Bunting, E. (1991). *The hideout*. New York: Trumpet.

Cassedy, S. (1985). *Behind the attic wall*. New York: Avon.

Christian, M. B. (1987). *Sebastian (super sleuth) and the stars-in-his eyes mystery*. New York: Macmillan.

Clymer, E. (1985). *The horse in the attic*. New York: Dell.

Cunningham, J. (1993). *Dorp dead*. New York: Knopf.

Giff, P. (1982). *Have you seen Hyacinth Macaw?* New York: Dell.

Hahn, M. D. (1988). *Following the mystery man.* New York: Clarion.

Hamilton, V. (1984). *The house of dies drear.* New York: Macmillan.

Hass, E. A. (1987). *Incognito mosquito makes history.* New York: Random House.

Howe, J. (1992). *Return to howliday inn.* New York: Avon.

Konigsburg, E. (1967). *From the mixed-up files of Mrs. Basil E. Frankweiler.* New York: Atheneum.

Konigsburg, E. (1974). *The dragon in the ghetto.* New York: Dell.

Landon, L. (1990). *Meg Mackintosh and the mystery at Camp Creepy.* Boston: Joy Street.

L'Engle, M. (1976). *Dragons in the water.* New York: Dell.

Miller, M. (1992). *You be the detective.* New York: Scholastic.

Monsell, M. E. (1989). *The mysterious cases of Mr. Pin.* New York: Atheneum.

Newman, R. (1981). *The case of the Baker Street irregular.* New York: Bantam.

Raskin, E. (1978). *The westing game.* New York: Avon.

Snyder, Z. K. (1967). *The Egypt game.* New York: Dell.

Sobol, D. (1986). *Two-minute mysteries.* New York: Scholastic.

Sobol, D. (1992). *Still more two-minute mysteries.* New York: Scholastic.

Stefanec-Ogren, C. (1989). *Sly P.I.: The case of the missing shoes.* New York: Harper.

Wallace, B. (1991). *Danger in quicksand swamp.* New York: Holiday House.

THEME 9: EXPLORATION

Teacher Resources

Computer Software

Discover space (IBM). Broderbund.

Spelunx and the caves of Mr. Suedo (Mac and IBM). Broderbund.

Where in space is Carmen Sandiego? (IBM). Broderbund.

Children's Resources

Children's Fiction Books

Cole, J. (1990). *The magic school bus: Lost in the solar system.* New York: Scholastic.

Schlein, M. (1991). *I sailed with Christopher Columbus.* New York: Trumpet.

Children's Nonfiction Books

Apfel, N. H. (1991). *Voyager to the Planets.* New York: Clarion.

Ballard, R. D. (1988). *Exploring the Titantic.* Lanham, MD: Madison Books.

Ballard, R. D. (1991). *Exploring the Bismarck: The real-life quest to find Hitler's greatest battleship.* New York: Scholastic.

Blassingame, W. (1979). *Thor Heyerdahl, Viking scientist.* Nashville, TN: Nelson Books.

Conley, A. (1991). *Window on the deep: Adventures of underwater explorer Sylvia Earle.* New York: Franklin Watts.

DeSomma, V. V. (1992). *The mission to Mars and beyond.* New York: Chelsea House Publishers.

Embury, B., & Crouch, T. D. (1991). *The dream is alive: A flight of discovery aboard the space shuttle.* New York: Harper Collins.

Fraser, M. A. (1991). *On top of the world: The conquest of Mount Everest.* New York: Henry Holt.

Henson, M. A. (1969). *A black explorer at the North Pole.* New York: Walker & Co.

Jefferis, D. (1988). *Epic flights: Trailblazing air routes.* New York: Watts.

Readers' Digest. (1978). *Great adventures that changed our world.* Pleasantville, NY: The Readers' Digest Association.

Schecter, D. (1979). *I can read all about Magellan.* New York: Troll.

Simon, S. (1986). *Stars.* New York: Morrow.

Westman, P. (1982). *Thor Heyerdahl: Across the seas of time.* Minneapolis: Dillon.

Book Sets

The World's Greatest Explorers Series. Chicago: Children's Press. Includes:

Vasco Nuñez de Balboa

Explorers of the Ancient World

Edmund Hillary

René-Robert Cavelier, Sieur de La Salle

Henry Stanley and David Livingstone

Ferdinand Magellan

Zebulon Pike

Roald Edmundsen and Robert Scott

THEME 10: THE ENVIRONMENT

Children's Resources

Children's Fiction Books

Baker, J. (1987). *Where the forest meets the sea.* New York: Greenwillow.

Cherry, L. (1990). *The great kapok tree.* New York: Trumpet.

George, J. C. (1990). *On the far side of the mountain.* New York: Trumpet.

Seuss, D. (1971). *The lorax.* New York: Random House.

Silverstein, S. (1964). *The giving tree.* New York: Harper & Row.

Van Allsburg, C. (1990). *Just a dream.* Boston: Houghton Mifflin.

Yolen, J. (1992). *Letting swift river go.* Boston: Little, Brown.

Children's Nonfiction Books

Ancona, G. (1990). *Riverkeeper.* New York: Macmillan.

Brown, J. E. (1978). *Oil spills: Danger in the sea.* Minneapolis, MN: Dodd, Mead.

Carr, T. (1991). *Spill! The story of the Exxon Valdez.* New York: Franklin Watts.

Earthworks Group. (1990). *Fifty simple things kids can do to save the earth.* Kansas City, MO: Andrews & McMeel.

Earthworks Group. (1991). *Kid heroes of the environment.* Berkeley, CA: Earthworks.

Foreman, M. (1991). *One world.* Boston: Arcade.

Hadingham, E., & Hadingham, J. (1990). *Garbage: Where it comes from, where it goes.* New York: Simon & Schuster.

Hare, T. (1990). *Acid rain.* New York: Gloucester Press.

Heilman, J. (1992). *Tons of trash: Why you should recycle and what happens when you do.* New York: Avon.

Johnson, R. L. (1990). *The greenhouse effect: Life on a warmer planet.* Minneapolis: Lerner Publications.

Landau, E. (1991). *Tropical rain forests around the world.* New York: Franklin Watts.

Miller, C. G., & Berry, L. A. (1986). *Wastes.* New York: Franklin Watts.

Seltzer, M. (1992). *Here comes the recycling truck!* Niles, IL: Albert Whitman.

Woods, G., & Woods, H. (1985). *Pollution.* New York: Franklin Watts.

THEME 11: HEROES AND HEROINES

Children's Resources

Children's Nonfiction Books

Angle, A. (1989). *John Glenn: Space pioneer.* New York: Fawcett.

Blacknall, C. (1984). *Sally Ride: America's first woman in space.* Minneapolis: Dillon Press.

Codye, C. (1990). *Luis W. Alvarez.* Milwaukee: Raintree Steck-Vaughn.

Davidson, M. (1988). *The story of Jackie Robinson, bravest man in baseball.* New York: Dell.

Davis, B. (1971). *Heroes of the American revolution.* New York: Random House.

Earthworks. (1991). *Kid heroes of the environment.* Berkeley, CA: Earthworks.

Faber, D. (1985). *Eleanor Roosevelt: First lady of the world.* New York: Viking Kestrel.

Foster, L. (1992). *Nien Cheng: Courage in China.* Chicago: Childrens.

Frommer, H. (1984). *Jackie Robinson.* New York: Franklin Watts.

Goodwin, D. (1991). *Cesar Chavez: Hope of the people.* New York: Fawcett.

Haskins, J. (1992). *The day that Martin Luther King, Jr. was shot.* New York: Scholastic.

Hudson, W., & Wesley, V. W. (1988). *Book of black heroes from a to z.* New York: Scholastic.

Hunter, E. F. (1963). *Child of the night: The story of Laura Bridgman.* Boston: Houghton Mifflin.

McGovern, A. (1975). *The secret soldier: The story of Deborah Sampson.* New York: Four Winds Press.

McMane, F., & Wolf, C. (1991). *The worst day I ever had.* New York: Sports Illustrated for Kids.

Rivinus, E. (1990). *Jim Thorpe.* Milwaukee: Raintree Steck-Vaughn.

Sloate, S. (1989). *Amelia Earhart: Challenging the skies.* New York: Fawcett.

THEME 12: TROLLS AND WITCHES

Children's Resources

Children's Fiction Books

Bellaire, J. (1984). *The spell of the sorcerer's skull.* New York: Dial.

Blacker, T. (1990). *Ms. Wiz spells trouble.* Hauppauge, NY: Barron's.

Corbett, S. (1985). *Witch hunt*. Boston: Little, Brown.

Jackson, S. (1956). *The witchcraft of Salem village*. New York: Random.

Konigsburg, E. (1967). *Jennifer, Hecate, Macbeth, William McKinley, and me, Elizabeth*. New York: Atheneum.

Kotzwinkle, W. (1978). *The leopard's tooth*. New York: Avon.

McKissack, P. C. (1992). *The dark-thirty: Southern tales of the supernatural*. New York: Knopf.

Naylor, P. R. (1975). *Witch's sister*. New York: Atheneum.

Rinaldi, A. (1992). *A break with charity: A story about the Salem witch trials*. Harcourt Brace Jovanovich.

Snyder, Z. K. (1972). *The witches of worm*. New York: Dell.

Tolan, S. S. (1992). *The witch of Maple Park*. New York: Morrow Junior Books.

Children's Nonfiction Books

Bird, M. (1988). *The witch's handbook*. New York: Aladdin.

Krensky, S. (1989). *Witch hunt: It happened in Salem*. New York: Random House.

Shaw, R., (Ed.). (1975). *Witch, witch! Stories and poems of sorcery, spells & hocus-pocus*. New York: Frederick Warne.

Teacher Resources

The resources included in this appendix are only a sampling of the many available for teachers and students. We have chosen those that have been most useful to us and to our students. Many of the chosen resources will provide you with information about how to obtain other books or information.

TECHNICAL ARTICLES

Colt, J. M. (1990). Support for new teachers in literature-based reading programs. *Journal of Reading, 34,* 64–66.

Freeman, E. B., & Levstik, L. (1988). Recreating the past: Historical fiction in the social studies curriculum. *Elementary School Journal, 88,* 329–337.

Hewitt, A. M., & Roos, M. C. (1990). *Thematic-based literature throughout the curriculum.* ERIC document: ED314718.

Huck, C. (1991). Literature and literacy. *Langauge Arts, 69,* 521–525.

McClure, A. A. (1982). Integrating children's fiction and informational literature in a primary reading curriculum. *The Reading Teacher, 35,* 784–789.

McGee, L. M. (1991). The literature-based revolution. *Language Arts, 69,* 529–537.

Pace, G. (1991). When teachers use literature for literacy instruction: Ways that constrain, ways that free. *Language Arts, 68,* 12–25.

Scharer, P. L. (1991). Moving into literature-based reading instruction: Changes and challenges for teachers. In J. Zutell & S. McCormick (Eds.), *Learner factors/teacher factors: Issues in literacy research and instruction.* Chicago: National Reading Conference.

PROFESSIONAL BOOKS

Atwell, N. (1987). *In the middle: Writing, reading, and learning with adolescents.* Portsmouth, NH: Boynton/Cook.

Atwell, N. (Ed.). (1990). *Coming to know: Writing to learn in the intermediate grades.* Portsmouth, NH: Heinemann.

Bromley, K. D. (1991). *Webbing with literature: Creating story maps with children's books.* Boston: Allyn and Bacon.

Butzow, C. M., & Butzow, J. W. (1989). *Science through children's literature.* Englewood, CO: Libraries Unlimited.

Charlesworth, R., & Lind, K. (1990). *Math and science for young children.* New York: Delmar.

Cullinan, B. E. (Ed.). (1987). *Children's literature in the reading program.* Newark, DE: International Reading Association.

Cullinan, B. E. (Ed.). (1992). *Invitation to read: More children's literature in the reading program.* Newark, DE: International Reading Association.

Cullinan, B. E. (Ed.). (1993). *Fact and fiction: Literature across the curriculum.* Newark, DE: International Reading Association.

Cullinan, B. E. (Ed.). (1993). *Pen in hand: Children become writers.* Newark, DE: International Reading Association.

Eisele, B. (1991). *Managing the whole language classroom.* Cypress, CA: Creative Teaching Press.

Graves, D. H. *Investigate nonfiction.* Portsmouth, NH: Heinemann, 1989.

Griffiths, R., & Clyne, M. (1991). *Books you can count on: Linking mathematics and literature.* Portsmouth, NH: Heinemann.

Hansen, J., Newkirk, T., & Graves, D. (Eds.). (1985). *Breaking ground: Teachers relate reading and writing in the elementary school.* Portsmouth, NH: Heinemann.

Hart-Hewins, L., & Wells, J. (1990). *Real books for reading: Learning to read with children's literature.* Portsmouth, NH: Heinemann.

Herr, J., & Libby, Y. (1990). *Creative resources for the early childhood classroom.* New York: Delmar.

Johnson, T., & Louis, D. (1987). *Literacy through literature.* Portsmouth, NH: Heinemann.

Moss, J. F. (1984). *Focus units in literature: A handbook for elementary school teachers.* Urbana, IL: National Council of Teachers of English.

Olson, M. W., & Homan, S. P., (Eds.). (1993). *Teacher to teacher: Strategies for the elementary classroom.* Newark, DE: International Reading Association.

Pappas, C. C., Kiefer, B. Z., & Levstik, L. S. (1990). *An integrated language perspective in the elementary school.* White Plains, NY: Longman.

Raines, S. C., & Canady, R. J. (1989). *Story s-t-r-e-t-c-h-e-r-s: Activities to expand children's favorite books.* Mt. Rainier, MD: Gryphon House.

Reasoner, C. F. (1975). *When children read: The third teacher's guide to Yearling Books.* New York: Dell.

Roettger, D. (1989). *Reading beyond the basal plus.* Logan, IA: The Perfection Form Co.

Routman, R. (1991). *Invitations: Changing as teachers and learners K–12.* Portsmouth, NH: Heinemann.

Saul, W., & Newman, A. R. (1986). *Science fare.* New York: Harper & Row.

Sisson, E. A. (1982). *Nature with children of all ages.* Englewood Cliffs, NJ: Prentice-Hall.

Somers, A. B., & Worthington, J. E. (1979). *Response guides for teaching children's books.* Urbana, IL: National Council of Teachers of English.

Thiessen, D., & Matthias, M. (Eds.). (1993). *The wonderful world of mathematics: A critically annotated list of children's books in mathematics.* Newark, DE: International Reading Association.

Trelease, J. (1985). *The read aloud handbook.* New York: Penguin Books.

Whitin, D. J., & Wilde, S. (1992). *Read any good math lately? Children's books for mathematical learning, K–6.* Portsmouth, NH: Heinemann.

RESOURCES RELATED TO ASSESSMENT

Anthony, R. J., Johnson, T. D., Mickelson, N. I., & Preece, A. (1991). *Evaluating literacy: A perspective for change.* Portsmouth, NH: Heinemann.

Batzle, J. (1992). *Portfolio assessment and evaluation: Developing and using portfolios in the K–6 classroom.* Cypress, CA: Creative Teaching Press.

Glazer, S. M., and Brown, C. S. (1993). *Portfolios and beyond: Collaborative assessment in reading and writing.* Norwood, MA: Christopher Gordon Publishers.

Harp, B. (Ed.). (1991). *Assessment and evaluation in whole language programs.* Norwood, MA: Christopher Gordon Publishers.

Herman, J. L., Aschbacher, P. R., & Winters, L. (1992). *A practical guide to alternate assessment.* Alexandria, VA: ASCD.

Hill, B. C., & Ruptic, C. A. (1993). *Practical aspects of authentic assessment: Putting the pieces together.* Norwood, MA: Christopher Gordon Publishers.

Johnson, P. H. (1992). *Constructive evaluate of literate activity.* White Plains, NY: Longman.

Marzano, R. J., Pickering, D., & McTighe, J. (1993). *Assessing student outcomes: Performance assessment using the dimensions of learning model.* Alexandria, VA: Association for Supervision and Curriculum Development.

Redesigning assessment series: Introduction, portfolios, performance. (1992). Video Series. Alexandria, VA: Association for Supervision and Curriculum Development.

Tierney, R. J., Carter, M. A., & Desai, L. E. (1991). *Portfolio assessment in the reading-writing classroom.* Norwood, MA: Christopher Gordon Publishers.

Valencia, S. (1990). A portfolio approach to classroom reading assessment: The whys, whats, and hows. *The Reading Teacher, 43,* 338–340.

MULTIMEDIA SOURCES

Reading Rainbow: Tapes and teacher's guides

GPN
P.O. Box 80669
Lincoln, NE 68501
(800) 228-4630

National Geographic Society: Videos
17th and M Streets
Washington, DC 20036

COMPUTER SOFTWARE

Appleworks
South-Western
5101 Madison Road
Cincinnati, OH 45227

Bank Street Prewriter
Scholastic
730 Broadway
New York, NY 10003

Bank Street Writer III
Broderbund Software-Direct
P.O. Box 6125
Novato, CA 94948-6125

FirstWriter
  Houghton Mifflin
  One Beacon Street
  Boston, MA 02108

Kid Pix and Kid Pix Companion
  Broderbund Software-Direct
  P.O. Box 6125
  Novato, CA 94948-6125

Kidwriter
  Spinnaker Software Corp.
  One Kendall Square
  Cambridge, MA 02139

Living Books (Macintosh)
  The tortoise and the hare told by Mark Schlichting
  In English and Spanish
  Broderbund Software-Direct
  P.O. Box 6125
  Novato, CA 94948-6125

Macmillan Writing Program
  Macmillan
  866 Third Avenue
  New York, NY 10022

Magic Slate
  Sunburst Communications
  39 Washington Street
  Pleasantville, NY 10570

Readable Classic Tales (Mac and IBM)
  Fas-track Computer Products
  Dept. F1,
  7030C Huntley Rd.
  Columbus, OH 43229

Spelunx and the Caves of Mr. Suedo (Mac and IBM)
  Broderbund Software-Direct
  P. O. Box 6125
  Novato, CA 94948-6125

Storybook Weaver (Mac)
  MECC Educational Resources
  1550 Executive Drive
  Elgin, IL 60123

Where in Space is Carmen Sandiego? and others (IBM)
  Broderbund Software-Direct
  P.O. Box 6125
  Novato, CA 94948-6125

Writing Workshop
  Milliken
  1100 Research Blvd.
  P.O. Box 21579
  St. Louis, MO 63132

REVIEWS OF CHILDREN'S BOOKS

Children's Choice Awards
  International Reading Association
  October issue of *The Reading Teacher*

Teachers' Choice Awards
  International Reading Association
  November issue of *The Reading Teacher*

The New Advocate
  Christopher Gordon Publishers
  480 Washington Street
  Norwood, MA 02062

School Library Journal
  249 West 17th St.
  New York, NY 10011

Language Arts
  National Council for Teachers of English
  1111 Kenyon Rd.
  Urbana, IL 61801

The Elementary School Paperback Collection
  American Library Association
  50 East Huron Street
  Chicago, IL 60611

Book Links
  American Library Association
  50 East Huron Street
  Chicago, IL 60611

Hornbook Magazine
  Park Square Bldg.
  31 St. James Ave.
  Boston, MA 02116

The WEB (Wonderfully Exciting Books)
Martha L. King Center for Language and Literacy
Ohio State University
29 Woodruff Ave.
Columbus, OH 43210-1177

A to zoo: Subject access to children's picture books
Bowker
121 Chanlon Road
New Providence, NJ 07974

Science book list for children
American Association for the Advancement of Science
1333 H. St. NW
Washington, DC 20005

CHILDREN'S MAGAZINES

Cobblestone: The History Magazine for Young People
Cobblestone Publishing
20 Grove Street
Peterborough, NH 03458

Crickett, The Magazine for Children
Box 51144
Boulder, CO 80321-1144
(800) BUG-PALS

Ladybug, The Magazine for Young Children
Cricket Country Lane
Box 50284
Boulder, CO 80321-0284
(800) BUG-PALS

Zoobook
P.O. Box 85384
San Diego, CA 92186-5384

Highlights for Children
Department CA
P.O. Box 182051
Columbus, OH 43218-2051

3-2-1 Contact
Children's Television Workshop
1 Lincoln Plaza
New York, NY 10023

National Geographic World
  Dept. 00683
  17th & M Streets NW
  Washington, DC 20036

Odyssey
  7 School Street
  Peterborough, NH 03458

Ranger Rick Nature Magazine
  1400 16th Street NW
  Washington, DC 20036

The Electric Company
  200 Watt Street
  P.O. Box 2924
  Boulder, CO 80322

Ebony Jr.!
  Johnson Publishing Co.
  820 S. Michigan
  Chicago, IL 60605

Chickadee
  Young Naturalist Foundation
  56 The Esplanada
  Suite 306
  Toronto, Ontario M5E1A7

Jack and Jill
  P.O. Box 1003
  Des Moines, IA 50340

Stone Soup
  The Magazine by Children
  P.O. Box 83
  Santa Cruz, CA 95063

Sesame Street
  P.O. Box 55518
  Boulder, CO 80322-5518

Your Big Backyard
  National Wildlife Federation
  1400 16th Street NW
  Washington, DC 20036

Zillions
  Consumers Union
  P.O. Box 54861
  Boulder, CO 80322

Sports Illustrated for Kids
  P.O. Box 830609
  Birmingham, AL 35283-0609

PROFESSIONAL JOURNALS

The Reading Teacher
International Reading Association, PO Box 8139, Newark, DE 19714-8139

The Journal of Reading
International Reading Association, PO Box 8139, Newark, DE 19714-8139

Language Arts
National Council of Teachers of English, 1111 Kenyon Road, Urbana, IL 61801

The Social Studies
National Council of Social Studies, 4000 Albemarle Street NW, Washington, DC 20016

The WEB
The Martha L. King Center for Language and Literacy, Ohio State University, 29 Woodruff Ave., Columbus, OH 43210-1177

Social Studies and the Young Learner
National Council for Social Studies, 4000 Albemarle Street NW, Washington, DC 20016

Arithmetic Teacher
National Council for Teachers of Mathematics, 1906 Association Drive, Reston, VA 22091

Mathematics Teacher
National Council for Teachers of Mathematics, 1906 Association Drive, Reston, VA 22091

Science and Children
National Science Teachers Association, 1742 Connecticut Avenue NW, Washington, DC 20009

The New Advocate
Christopher Gordon Publishers, Norwood, MA

GLOSSARY

Attitude objectives Dispositions encouraged or developed during a unit of study.

Authentic assessment Determining student strengths and weaknesses in the context of daily learning activities.

Authentic children's literature Stories and informational text written by professional authors expressly for enjoyment or to provide information.

Authentic experiences Activities modeled after real-life experiences, such as classroom banking or letter writing.

Brainstorming A creative process in which all ideas related to a specific topic are expressed.

Concepts Primary or "big" ideas selected from content areas.

Concluding activities Activities that bring closure to the unit or lesson and that allow students to demonstrate what they have learned.

Developing activities Activities that compose the major part of the unit and provide students with a variety of experiences.

Explicit instruction Teacher-directed lessons.

External motivation The use of tangible rewards such as stickers or prizes to encourage a child to become an active learner.

Focus The specific emphasis of a unit; a well-defined framework that allows children to make connections among ideas, concepts, and experiences. Specifically in this text, *focus* refers to a topic from a content area, a single piece of literature, or a combination of concepts and children's literature.

Inclusion model   Refers to the practice of providing instruction for learners with special needs within the regular classroom.

Informational text   Same as nonfiction text.

Initiating activities   Activities designed to activate students' prior knowledge of a topic and to stimulate interest in the study.

Internal motivation   An inner drive to learn that results in personal satisfaction and a continuous pursuit of knowledge.

Journals   A written collection of reflections based on personal reading and writing experiences.

Knowledge objectives   Specific concepts or information to be learned during a unit of study.

Learning logs   A collection of an individual student's written responses to content activities and instruction.

Literacy   The ability of children to use reading, writing, listening, speaking, and viewing processes in real-life settings.

Literacy-rich environment   An environment that provides opportunities for engagement with print and nonprint resources.

Literature-based instruction   Instruction in which children use literature (tradebooks and information books) as a source of information and pleasure.

Mandated curriculum   Instructional objectives, concepts, and/or materials required by local or state educational agencies.

Minilesson   A ten- to fifteen-minute teacher-directed lesson on a single strategy or concept based upon specific needs of students related to unit objectives.

Model (1)   An instructional design based on the purpose of the unit; literature supplement model, literature-centered model, or literature-infused model; (2) To explicitly demonstrate a strategy or process.

Peer evaluation   Students' evaluation of one another's participation and/or work samples.

Planning web   A graphic representation of concepts, activities, and resources used in initial development of a unit.

Portfolio assessment   Pieces of evidence, selected and collected by the student and teacher, which are used to document student learning.

Prepackaged units   Commercially packaged modules containing activities and/or lessons revolving around a single topic.

Process objectives Skills and strategies that are emphasized during a unit of study.

Scaffolding   Instructional support that is gradually released as the learner becomes more independent in the learning process.

Schema   Unique experiences and understandings of concepts that each individual brings to a learning task.

Self-evaluation   Students' reflections on their own contributions.

Skills-based classroom   A classroom setting in which skill mastery is the primary objective.

Strategies   Techniques students and teachers use to apply knowledge and attitudes in new contexts.

Teacher evaluation   Assessment designed and implemented by the teacher.

Thematic unit   A unit that is the result of a process in which learning experiences are organized around a central focus. The focus may be a piece of literature, a content area topic, or a set of integrated concepts and selections of children's literature.

Tradebooks   Literature, fiction or informational, that is available on the commercial market.

INDEX

O

P

R

S

T

Notes

Notes

Notes

Notes

Notes

Notes

Notes

Notes

Notes

Notes

Notes

Notes

Notes

Notes

Notes

Notes

Notes

Notes